The Evolution of the Pictish Legend

DF Dale B.Eng(Hons)

Preface

My first book "The History of the Scots, Picts and Britons" was the end result of a problem I had with the ancient Scots, or rather the accepted view of their origins. The problem was this – the academic view, from the studies conducted by William F. Skene and later is that the Scots migrated from Ireland into Argyll around the 5th Century AD and from this small foothold, they conquered, or at least gained control of, the Northern part of Britain by the 9th - 10th Century. The problems with this view are many, the earliest Scots traditions claim that they migrated from Ireland many hundreds of years earlier, more importantly the only archaeological evidence we have of Irish settlement in Scotland occurs in the South West of the country, also hundreds of years earlier than the 5th century, Other than in prehistoric times, Argyll shows no evidence of any settlement from Ireland either before, during or after the 5th Century. The first accepted king of Scotland, Kenneth McAlpin, emerges not from Argyll or the North West, but from the Galloway region in South West Scotland.

This led me to the natural conclusion that the Scots did not settle Argyll, they settled in South Western Scotland and it was from the region of Strathclyde that they began their expansion into the North. This conclusion meant that I had to review my understanding of the Roman Occupation, the wars of the dark ages and the emergence of the associated peoples and kingdoms of ancient Britain. Eventually, after many years of procrastination, my first book was written.

I did not intend to write another book but have recently found myself drawn more and more into the mysterious world of the Picts. The Picts, traditionally, in modern terms anyway, are thought to be a warlike, ancient pre-Celtic people, they occupied most of what is now Scotland, They tattooed their bodies, in readiness for warfare, worshipped strange gods, had a now extinct language of which there are few, if any, traces. They fought the Romans in brutal conflicts and helped to drive them out of ancient Britain. Eventually they, their beliefs, language, religion and practices all disappeared completely, sometime between the emergence of Kenneth McAlpin in the 9th Century and the death of MacBeth in the mid 11th Century, and they have left little or no traces, save for a few obscure place-names and a collection of pictures cut into stone obelisks.

That is the accepted view of the Picts, but like the Scots there are huge unavoidable problems. We have knowledge now of what really happens when peoples are conquered and how violently and religiously they fight to retain their identity and culture, not just over a few years but over hundreds, even thousands of years – for example the Wars of Scottish Independence in the late 13th and early 14th century, and in more modern times, the Nationalist cause still prevalent in Scottish politics more than 300 years after the 1707 Act of Union, The Irish, conquered by the Anglo Norman English in the early medieval period, and the violence of their struggle for home rule hundreds of years later in the 19th and 20th Century, The Welsh, conquered by Edward I in the late 13th century, still striving for self determination and keeping their culture and language alive almost 1000 years later. And what about the Native Americans, The Aborigines of Australia, The Maories of New Zealand, not to mention the Catalans, and the Basques of Spain and the brutal violence of the rebellions in India and Africa as they also struggled to break free of their Colonial oppression.

These people fought for and maintained their culture and heritage, in spite of huge, almost insurmountable pressures, both political and military. The experiences of warfare over the past thousand years proves that violence and oppression does not drive out resistance or suppress culture, it makes it stronger and it's defence more extreme – we only need look at the 20th century and the freedom fighters of Poland, France, Holland, Norway, the bloody resistance of the Russians at Stalingrad and Leningrad, and the sacrifice of the lives of millions of men, women and children during the 2nd World War to see evidence of this.

It is the Picts that are the odd ones out – they almost completely abandoned their heritage, culture and language without a whimper or shout of complaint – relatively speaking, one moment they were there and the next, they had completely vanished. What is even more surprising is that they were the majority and not the minority of the population.

This is the mystery of the Picts, not who they were, what their language was or even where they originated from, but the reasons for the rapid abandonment of their heritage. This is what I hope to answer in this book.

Index

- Preface
- introduction
- The Historical Evidence
- Alcluith and The Early Maps
- The Pictish King List
- The Appearance of the Pict
- The Pictish Religion
- A Combined Symbol
- An Indigenous Population
- Problems and Contradictions
- The Epidi – a lost Pictish/Scottish tribe
- The Evolution of Roman Britain
- The Evolution of the Picts
- Summary
- Bibliography

Introduction

The Picts are an enigma., no-one really knows much about them or their origins, as a result, there have been numerous assumptions by many learned and unlearned men and women. Either they are a Brythonic people or the descendants of indigenous prehistoric inhabitants of northern Britain.

In Irish legends they are migrants and when they arrived in Britain they were short of females and sought wives from the native Irish. Upon granting this request they were then compelled to always select their monarchs from the female line. This is often used as the justification for the statement in Bede's Ecclesiastical history that they selected their kings from the maternal rather than the paternal line. It also becomes the vehicle for justification of the claims of Irish/Scottish kinship with the Picts and eventual overlordship over them.

The contemporary evidence relies on 4 rather limited testimonies from Roman historians, 2 angry monks whose intention was to berate their own leaders and 1 monk whose purpose was really propaganda. After that we are left with some rather fantastical and outrageous legends which were written down hundreds of years after the "historical" events they are supposed to describe.

Some writers consider the Picts to be the descendants of a prehistoric people, possibly the same people that built the structures at Skara Brae in Orkney and the Pibrochs of Northern Scotland. However the earliest point in time that we can date them to is around 297AD, when the writer Eumenius writes a panegyric in praise of the Roman Emperor Constantius Chlorus. There is no mention of them in the earlier works by Julius Caesar and Tacitus. This occurs long after Skara Brae and the Brochs were constructed and abandoned.

Under Roman Occupation we only know for certain of 3 tribes that were linked to the Picts – the Caledones, The Verturiones and the DiCalydones.. Tribes like the Cornavi, the Lugi, the Dumnoni of Strathclyde are not mentioned amongst the Roman testimonies, yet we know they were present in Scotland, thanks to the 2nd Century Geographia written down by the Greek writer Ptolomey.

In the period just before, and after the end of Roman Occupation, between the 4th and 9th Centuries AD we begin to see the creation of the most familiar and prolific of Pictish Objects – the stone monuments with the rod and Z form inscriptions, battle scenes, symbols that we do not yet fully understand. Yet they appear to be concentrated in the north east of the Scottish mainland. In the Lowland and Central regions of Scotland, there is very little, if any, evidence of these monuments.

The end of the Picts is also somewhat of a mystery. Kenneth McAlpin was traditionally seen as the first Scots King to gain control of the Pictish territories on Northern Britain around 843AD. But it was not until not his grandson Domnall Mac Constantine's death c.900AD, that his descendants stopped being known as Kings of the Picts and became known as Kings of Alba. We know that by 1140AD the Picts had ceased to exist as people when Henry of Huntingdon tells us that

"The Picts however have entirely disappeared and their language is extinct"

so in less than 240 years the Picts had been wiped from history. If the Picts had existed for several thousand years, this is a remarkably short period of time for an entire people, traditions and language to disappear. The time period may even be less than that, as Kenneth McAlpin's reign began in c. 843AD, but he was called a King of Picts throughout his tenure. It was around 900AD that this title ceases to be used when his grandson Domnall's death is recorded. At the start of Domnall's reign c. 889AD, he was called King of Picts, but by 900AD when he dies his title has changed to King of Alba. That is 11 years between the start of his reign and it's end - 11 years in which a people disappear from history – a remarkably short period of time.

In Empire times, whether Victorian, Roman, Holy Roman, Italian, French, Austrian, Hungarian etc., there is a simple belief and an assumption that under conquest a people can be "re-educated", have their history rewritten and become assimilated into the new Empire. In real terms, this belief is entirely false – The Britons, Gauls, Visigoths revolted against their Roman "Conquerors" repeatedly, the Indians, Boers, Africans etc. revolted against the British Empire. The Aborigines, Maories, Native Americans revolted against their "overlords", The Cossacks revolted against the Poles, The Swiss against the Austrians etc.

Even under a political alliance, the Scots refused to accept being described as North Britons after the 1707 act of Union, and have, some 300 years after it was voluntarily disbanded, reinstated a national parliament. The Welsh although conquered by Edward I, have striven almost continuously to preserve their national identity and language for hundreds of years, and I have not yet mentioned the Irish question that dominated political and military events over the 19th and 20th Century. The culmination of which was that by the end of the 20th Century, recognition of their national identities has been accepted politically, with a national assembly for Wales and the unique situation of an assembly in Northern Ireland and an independent state in the Republic of Ireland. In these cases, the political leaders of each country had willingly abandoned their allegiances, accepted the new order and became participants in the attempts to reduce their countries to regions, and remove Scots, Welsh and Irish as a national identity., It was the general population that resisted it and continued to maintain a belief in their national identity and traditions.

In short if a collective of people have a sense of a national identity, allied to a language that is unique to themselves, it would be an almost insurmountable problem to get them to accept or adopt a new identity. This is what makes the Picts unique – between 889AD and 1140 AD, they had completely given up on their identity, their language and their culture. The question is why?.

To answer this question we have to look further at their origins, and their evolution into Medieval Scots

Chaper1: The Historical Evidence

In the years following the Roman Occupation, starting around 43AD, we get to find out a bit more about the people of Britain and their often violent relationship with their new overlords. Starting with a few brief pieces of information we gradually begin to find out more over the course of the following 5/6 centuries from first Roman, then British, European, Irish and English sources – each source adding something new to the tale.

Our knowledge and view of the of the Picts is a result of adding all of the testimonies together. However we never hear from the Picts themselves, the evidence that we are given contains a large number of difficulties and contradictions, which are summarised in the following sections.

Eumenius & Tacitus

In 297AD we get out first known reference to the Picts. It is in a poem by the writer Eumenius in praise of the Emperor Constantius Chlorus, and tells of how in Julius Caesar's day

"a nation, still savage and accustomed to the hitherto semi-naked Picts and Hibernians as their enemies, yielded to to Roman Arms and standards without difficulty"

There are a number of interesting points to note here that are missing from, or contrary to, Eumenius' claims.

1. There is no location given for these Picts
2. We see the Picts and Hibernians (Scots) mentioned together for the first time
3. The Britons did not yield to Caesar at all – they fought him off and eventually, he returned to Rome,

having secured only a token agreement for tribute.
4. At no point in his much earlier biography does Julius Caesar mention that there were Picts harassing Britons around 54BC.

Clearly Eumenius is talking to an audience in his time period and exaggerating events from Julius' Caesar's time to make his hero more appealing. We have 3 problems;

1. The Romans had been present in Britain for some 250 years. They first landed in Britain at an even earlier point in time around 54BC. Julius Caesar got information about Britain first hand from the druid Divitacus in the 1st century BC, stating the interior of Britain was indigenous and in the coastal regions were later Belgic settlers. In the 1st century AD the general Agricola travelled the length and breadth of Britain, fought the battle of Mons Grapius in the North of Britain against the war leader Calgacus yet there is no mention in Agricola's biography, of the name Pict or Picti. The author, Tacitus, probably accompanied Agricola on his travels, so why not?

2. Many writers claim that the Picts were the indigenous people of Britain, arriving from "Scythia" meaning Scandinavia, via the Orkneys. There is archaeological evidence from recent excavations carried out at Stonehenge, that travellers from the far North of Britain did make their way South to join up with other southern tribes for shared ritual festivals or ceremonies in the prehistoric period, but there is no mention of a prehistoric Pictish population in the early sources. There is evidence from Tacitus that he had made enquiries about "aboriginal" inhabitants of Britain, and found numerous contenders vying to be named as such, when he uses the following phrase -

"who the first inhabitants of Britain were, whether natives or immigrants is open to question...But their physical characteristics vary, and the variation is suggestive. The reddish hair and large limbs of the Caledonians proclaim a German origin; the swarthy faces of the Silures, the tendency of their hair to curl, and the fact that Spain lies opposite, all lead one to believe that Spaniards crossed in ancient times and occupied that part of the country. The peoples nearest to the Gauls likewise resemble them".

Tacitus does not mention that any one of these groups, including the Caledonians, were related to other tribes or arrived with any other tribes under the banner of the name of Pict.

3. Eumenius writes about contemporary events, he does not mention anything about Picts being painted or tattooed or having any otherwise unusual appearance in comparison to the Hibernians – he describes both as "semi-naked". This means there is no difference in the behaviour or appearance between the Celtic tribes of Ireland and the Picts of Britain. This would eliminate the notion that the Picts were called Picts due to their "painted" appearance. Most likely is that they dressed and behaved exactly as native British Celts did prior to the Roman invasion and did not adopt Roman style dress and customs.

Ptolomey

In the 2nd century AD the Greek geographer Ptolomey mapped out the tribes of Britain. In the following diagram we can name the 18 tribes of Scotland and the surrounding Islands.

This leads us to our 4th problem

- Why is there no mention of the word Pict or anything similar to it in the names of any tribes or regions of Britain?

The Unknown Roman Author

Later testimonies by Roman writers and the 10th century Pictish Kings list (from the Pictish Chronicle, a 14th century manuscript that appears to be a copy of an earlier 10th century document), have led us to the conclusion that the Picts were made up of several tribes. The first evidence of this appears around 310AD in another panegyric, by an unknown writer, to Constantius where it mentions

"The Caledonians and other Picts"

So the first tribe that we can name for certain in the Picts is that of the Caledoni, or Caledonians. It has taken over 350 years for the Romans to mention any particular tribe as being Pict.

The statement is our first real evidence that there were Picts in the North of Britain, but it still gives us our fifth problem.

- The Caeldoni are a Northern tribe, we know this thanks to Ptolomey, but the names and locations of other Pictish tribes are not mentioned. The earlier evidence by Eumenius told us that the Picts were causing trouble for the Emperor Constantius Chlorus, but it didn't tell us exactly, where or why this took place. The mention of a northern tribe in this later statement, has led us to assume it was all taking place around or beyond the "Wall" - either Antonine, or Hadrian's. In actual fact there is nothing yet that suggests that all of the Pictish tribes were Northern based. Constantius, like many Emperors before and after him, experienced problems with native British tribes inside and outside Roman controlled territories, so there is nothing yet that limits the presence of Pictish tribes to the Northern regions only.

Ammianus Marcellinus

Around 360AD Ammianus Marcellinus gives us his testimony about "Scythian" tribes coming from Northern

Europe, and this time he got it from the religious leaders of the Celtic communities he was in contact with;

"that part of the population was in fact indigenous, but was joined by newcomers from remote islands and the country <u>beyond</u> the Rhine"

This sounds almost conclusive, or at least provides strong evidence of a "Pictish" people, not Belgic, but arriving from beyond the Rhine - "Scythia", creating our sixth problem

- This is similar to the sequence of settlement in early medieval British and Irish legends, where Picts arrive later and take the lands from the native Britons. This testimony has nothing to do with Britons however, this is the history of the Gallic Drysidae. Settlers from "beyond the Rhine" migrating into Southern Europe, and the name Pict is not mentioned. The story of "Picts" from Scythia appears to belong to the Gauls of France, and these were not "Picts" but La Tene era Celts and/or Germanic tribes. Our esteemed dark age and early medieval historians, Gildas, Bede, Nennius et al appear to have "adopted" the testimony of Ammianus Marcellinus and incorrectly applied it to a British Isles context.

Ammianus Marcellinus appears to have formed a relationship with the religious leaders of the Celtic Communities. We can see further evidence of this in other statements he makes such as;

"Hercules the son of Amphitryon"

who was the father of many sons that gave their names to the various Celtic tribes proves that he had also obtained an understanding of their beliefs, and that these religious leaders knew there was a discrepancy between the origin legends, and the reality of the settlement pattern. This is now our seventh problem

- For someone with an interest in the background and history of the Gauls, he fails to mention the origins of the population of the British Isles. He simply does not mention any British tribes as indigenous or a later incoming population. The earlier writer, Tacitus left this open to debate who the first settlers were – indicating it was either forgotten or wasn't that important to the native Britons. Ammianus Marcellinus, doesn't mention indigenous groups in Britain or anyone claiming to be this group. This supports the notion that no-one in Britain knew, or possibly cared, at that time who the first settlers were. This would go against the notion that the Picts were an indigenous group, or the modern assumption that Pict derives from a word "Pecht" meaning ancestor – quite simply it doesn't look like any one tribe is claiming this "honour" at all.

Apart from raiding, the only thing that Ammianus can tell us about the ethnicity of the Picts is that they are divided into 2 different groups.

"*The DiCalydones and the Verturiones*"

And this is our eighth problem.

- This splitting into 2 groups indicates that these 2 groups had a feature that made them different from each other. If the Picts were northern tribes, they would be living nearby each other, sharing the same origins, beliefs and customs, so why did they bother to separate into 2 groups. Far from being a single ethnic group, there are features that separate these groups – there is a fundamental difference in their make up that the "Pictish" tribes have used to align them to one of these 2 groups. The Picts do not all belong to the same "family", so they cannot have the same origins, but what was that feature?

Claudian Claudianus

The next person to mention the Picts was another Roman writer Claudian Claudianus. Who in praise of the 4th century general Stilicho, talks of Britain at that time being

"clothed in the skin of a Caledonian Beast, her cheeks tattooed, a deep blue cloak sweeping down to her feet"

This is the second reference to Caledoni, but this indicates that the "Caledonian" influence was stretching down to the very reaches of Southern Britain. We do know from the writer Zosimus that in the 3rd and 4th centuries, Native Britons had been under serious pressure and through a force of arms had regained a form of independence from Rome. This statement appears to attribute the pressure on Roman Britain to a Caledonian influence from the North.

One of the problems (our ninth) that Claudianus does bring us relates to the way in which the native Britons had been kept in check during the Roman rule. In the following phrase, while praising Stilicho. He claims that

"thanks to his care, I need not fear the arms of the Scots, nor tremble at the Picts, nor keep watch on all the shores for the coming of the Saxons"

This is one of the first times that we get the impression of a Saxon-Pict-Scot incursion into British territory, something which turns up later in the 9th century Historia Britonium by Nennius.

However the phrase may not be all that is seems. The Greek historian Zosimus, writing a History of the Roman Empire around 490-510AD provided some additional information about the way the Romans controlled the native population of Britain In his history he explains that captured barbarians from the Germania/Rhine regions were brought to Britain in the mid 3rd century AD by the Emperor Probus.

"the Romans challenged the Barbarians that were on the further side to fight….and fought until the Barbarians were all either slain or taken by the Romans……All of them that were taken alive were sent to Britain, where they settled, and were subsequently very serviceable to the emperor when any insurrection broke out".

The purpose of resettling these people here was to keep down the insurgencies by Native Britons. Claudianus' phrase may mean that before Stilicho came to Britain, it was under sustained violent attacks by Scots, Picts and Saxons together, but it may also be interpreted that Britain was watching anxiously on the shores for the Germanic "Saxons" to arrive and keep down the insurgent Picts and Scots.

A Tattooed People?

It is in the following phrase that we get our first mention of a possible practice of tattooing by the Picts when Claudianus mentions

"the strange shapes tattooed on the faces of the dying Picts"

However the phrase can be translated alternatively as;
"the strange shapes iron marked on the faces of the dying Picts"

This could alter our belief quite substantially - iron marked may just mean that they had adopted some form of headgear/helmet to protect their heads and faces during warfare. Perhaps it left marks or indentations in their skin when it was removed. That would not be so unusual – the Roman army wore some form of protective headgear, why wouldn't their enemies, who, after fighting them for some 350 years, may have done the same.

There may even be another explanation – the Roman army used mercenaries for fighting – perhaps it was a reference to the faces of the Picts being mutilated by the "iron" swords of Stilicho's troops as they lay dying.

It would also alter the earlier description of Britain as well instead of her cheeks being tattooed, this would read as;

"*her cheeks iron marked*"

At the time of the Roman invasion, Britain was in the midst of the iron age. This was the material of choice for the native inhabitants. By describing Britain in human form, the cheeks would be placed in the north – "the face" - that part of Britain that the Roman Army struggled to control.

This is now our tenth problem

- It has now taken 400 years since the Romans launched their successful invasion of Britain, for a description to arise of the Picts which may indicate that they practised "tattooing". Tacitus presented a much earlier, contemporary description of the Caledoni, a tribe that in the 3rd and 4th centuries were described as Picts. Tacitus described their appearance, colouring and possible Germanic origins, but failed to mention any such practice.

The literal phrase used by Claudianus is "iron marked" and this may just mean that they used iron quite extensively to decorate their weaponry in readiness for going into battle with the Roman legions.

St Patrick

Our first native British testimony regarding the Picts comes from the legendary St Patrick, in the middle of the 5th century. Patrick was a real person, captured around the age of 16 in mainland Britain and sold as a slave in Ireland. He later managed to obtain his freedom and returned to Britain. He travelled to Gaul where he trained as a Priest and eventually returned to Ireland, where his reputation developed into mythical status. While practising as a missionary in Ireland, Patrick wrote a very angry letter to the Strathclyde King Coroticus (Ceretic). In it he gives us some information about the Picts. He, like the Roman writers before him, indicates there was an alliance of some kind between the Scots and the Picts, which also involved the soldiers of Coroticus, when he describes the soldiers as

"allies of the apostate Scots and Picts"

This is a quite unexpected turn of events. Often we are given the impression that the Picts and Scots were operating against the Britons. In this case we see them as operating with Britons, Far from being enemies, they are working together.

But of more interest is another phrase that he uses later on to describe the fate of those Christians that had been captured and sold

"Christians reduced to slavery: slaves particularly of the lowest and worst of the apostate Picts"

His letter originally began telling us that the Scots were apostate and now we see that at least some of The Picts were also apostate – i.e. they had been Christian and had now returned to a pagan religion. This leads to our eleventh problem regarding the Picts

- This indicates that the Picts were not sharing the same religions, some had converted to Christianity, some had now reconverted back to a pagan religion. Had those that reconverted back, gone back to a Pre-Roman Pictish religion or had they taken on another religion instead.

Logic says the latter, for some their old gods would have appeared to have failed them when the Romans invaded, Some had taken on the new Christian religion, A subset of this group have subsequently rejected the new Christian teachings that they had formerly embraced. Seeking a more effective set of Gods, it makes sense that this subgroup would have adopted a new religion. We could have 3 different religions in operation amongst the Picts. This does not support the notion of a unified Pictish society, as by the middle of the 5th Century the Picts, as well as being divided into at least 2 groups were also now divided in their beliefs.

In any society, as we can see today, differences in belief systems, often leads to very serious outbreaks of violence, with bloody confrontations taking place between ethnic groups, and even individual family members. This makes it extremely unlikely that the Picts were a single unified people.

Gildas

After Patrick our next source is another British writer, the monk Gildas, who around the mid 6th century AD, describes both the Picts and the Scots, as

"*overseas*"

There is an argument that the Scots were raiders from Ireland so were based "overseas", however archaeological discoveries would contradict this statement. There is evidence of a flourishing trade taking place between South Western Scotland and the North of Ireland between the 6th century BC - 1st Century AD. Evidence of a population movement from Ireland to Scotland has been found in the Solway-Clyde region, with discoveries of neolithic Irish style pottery and axes. Crannogs (man-made lakeside dwellings) similar to those built by early Irish Celts have been found as far as Oakbank (Perthshire), that date to the 6th century BC. This places the "Scots" as settled in mainland Britain during the period that Gildas was writing about.

We must accept that the Picts were present in Northern Britain, at this time also. We have contemporary evidence for this from an unknown Roman writer who writes around 310AD that the Caledoni, mentioned by Ptolomey in the 2nd Century AD, were in fact Picts. So neither the Scots or the Picts could be geographically described as being "overseas". To try and reconcile the use of the term overseas for both, there may be an argument that Gildas is only talking of Britannia superior, i.e. Roman occupied Britain, but at the start of his discourse Gildas begins with his description Britain as 800 miles long, which is indeed, more or less, the length of Britain, from John O' Groats to Lands End so he is not using the term "overseas" in a geographical sense. This is our twelfth problem.

- The use of the term "overseas" by Gildas is in relation to a feature that the Scots and Picts both share. This feature is that they both originate from foreign shores, reaching the British mainland, long after the native Britons. Gildas provides our first native British testimony, written around the time that the "Pictish" kingdoms start to emerge, and he confidently makes a statement that the Picts were later "interlopers".

This claim of a late "Pictish arrival" agrees with Bede, Nennius and the Irish traditions. These traditions were made in the eighth, ninth and 10th centuries, also contemporary with the existence of Pictish society in Britain. This claim is unchallenged and not argued with, so we can deduce that the Picts themselves agreed with this view that their society were late arrivals to the shores of Britain. The Picts therefore also believed that they were not indigenous to the country. This is another contradiction to the theory of the Picts being amongst the original settlers of Britain.

Isidore of Seville

Isidore of Seville provides our next description of the Picts in the 6th/7th century AD, and it is from his testimony that we obtain our first link between the name Pict and the practice of "tattooing"

"The race of Picts has a name derived from the appearance of their bodies"

He then goes on to describe how they use a needle and the squeezed out sap of a native plant to mark themselves according to their rank.

But his evidence is the thirteenth problem -This practice, is a statement about something that is supposed to have occurred in the past and for which Isidore has no contemporary evidence. His testimony shows a knowledge of tattooing, but this was clearly gained from another non-British source.

Another problem – the fourteenth - with the practice is that of the availability of the natural resources to create the dyes. The 3 most common plants used for dyes would be Woad, Weld and Madder.

There is no evidence of any large scale production or availability in Scotland of these plants. Weld, which produces a yellow dye, was available around Perthshire and North East Scotland, but the other 2 would have to be imported from Southern Britain (the Midlands and Southern England), both areas that were under Roman control. A series of essays by Grigson and Dickson and Dickson pointed to a lack of evidence supporting the use of dyes by either Celts or Picts. It would seem that Isidore adopted the "iron marked" terminology of earlier Roman writers, then interpreted this to mean literally "painted" and thereby associating it to the name given to Northern British tribes during the Roman period of occupation.

This is now our fifteenth problem

- It has taken around 600 years or more for the relationship between the word Pict and their appearance to be linked together and for this to be related to the Latin word for "painted".. The Romans had abandoned Britain around 200 years earlier and Isidore has no first hand source available to substantiate the claim.

The association with the appearance to the practice of tattooing is not contemporary with the practices employed by "Pictish" people during Isidore's lifetime, nor is it supported by the availability of resources or archaeological evidence that such a practice was carried out in North Britain, either during or before the Roman invasion. This means that the name Pict cannot be a Roman term meaning "painted" and must derive from a native source.

Adomnan

Our next view of the Picts is in the Life of Columba, written in the 7th Century AD by Adomnan. The details are scarce but he describes the meeting between Columba and Breide Mac Maelcon in some detail. From this we gather than Breide employs a Druid, and by referring to this, Adomnan is highlighting that the Picts were holding onto Pagan Celtic practices.

Breide is ambivalent towards Columba, other later legends tell us of attacks by fierce Pictish warriors, which seems at odds with the nature of Breide's attitude towards Columba, which indicates a tolerance, of the burgeoning Christian religion, if not acceptance of the spread of Christianity amongst their communities. It indicates that the Pictish leaders have a realisation that there is a political benefit in avoiding confrontation with the early Celtic church.

But of more significance is the prophesy that Columba makes of the Dal Riadic (Scottish) King Aidan Mac Gabran's son Eochaid Bhuide, the yellow haired child, who Columba predicts will succeed Aidan, and take over control of the Pictish kingdom and reign in Fortrenn – the heart of Pictish power.

But these statements give us our 16th, 17th, 18th, 19th, 20th1 and 21st problems.
- Unlike the Roman sources, St Patrick and Gildas. Adomnan is not writing a contemporary account of people in his lifetime. His story is filled with some

fantastically impossible stories – such as the pebble that Columba gives to the Druid, or Magi, Briochan to cure him. Columba died c.597AD and, Adomnan wrote the Life of Columba after he became the ninth Abbot of Iona, so it dates to sometime after 679AD, over 80 years after Columba's death and after 7 abbots have preceded him. It is not remotely possible that there was anyone still alive that had first hand knowledge of any of the events in Adomnan's tale. A lot of it is clearly based on hearsay and legend, and probably mixed in with local pagan beliefs. It is very heavily embellished with fables, and probably, like St Patrick, has become mixed up with tales belonging to other mythical figures.

- The purpose of the story is to demonstrate the divinity of Columba – it was not written as a history of early Scotland; Like the old adage says when the "legend becomes fact, print the legend" and that is exactly what Adomnan did. The places, events and tales have to be taken with a "pinch of salt".

- It provides evidence that, the early Celtic church was striving to gain some political influence amongst the Northern Kingdoms and using legendary figures to create the impression of a former relationship. As well as visiting the Pictish King, Columba also attends Aidan MacGabhran, the Dalriadic King and Rydderich Hael, the Strathclyde King.

The tale really wasn't about events in the sixth century, more than likely it was intended for a seventh century audience, with some political undertones.

There was a conflict between the Northumbrian

Church and the Celtic Church in Iona. The Northumbrian Church had been formed as part of the early Celtic Church and it's development was led from Iona, where it was viewed as one if it's satellite churches. The early Saints in the Northumbrian Church were Northern based, St Cuthbert, a Strathclyde monk founded it according to legend, but it was St Aidan of Iona that had set up the structure and administration.

This changed after the Synod of Whitby in 662AD, when the Celtic church lost the debate regarding the calculation of Easter. The Celtic churches in the North continued with their own calculation of Easter, tonsure and style of worship, while the Northumbrian Church adopted the Gallic Church practices. This meant the 2 churches were subsequently competing for the religious control of the North.

In 685AD, while Adomnan was still the Abbot of Iona, an opportunity to gain an advantage arose, which he probably grasped with both hands. The Northumbrian king Ecgfrith was defeated by the Pictish King Breide Mac Bili, This is supposed to have "freed" the Picts from domination by Northumbria, but in reality, this meant a dramatic reduction in the Northumbrian Church influence in the North.

The visit of Columba to an earlier Pictish king, conversions of Picts to Christianity, the "magic pebble" that cured the Druid, and it's continued presence in the Pictish King's possession, is designed to give the impression of a continuing unbroken link between the Ionian Celtic Church, The Pictish kings and the development of Christianity in

"Pictland". The tale has to be seen as political and not historical.

Ironically the situation appeared to have gone against the Ionian Church c.705AD when the Pictish King Nechton subsequently adopted the Roman Calculation of Easter for his church. This would not have happened on a whim, or through divine intervention, so it provides evidence of political manoeuvring in the early Churches, probably through gifts, "bribes" etc. being offered and accepted. There is a power struggle going on between the Churches in the North of Britain.

- The location of Breide Mac Maelcon's capital is not mentioned at all. There is a belief that the capital is near Inverness due to the legend of Columba saving his follower Luigne mocco Muin from a water beast in the River Ness, which has often been associated with the tale of the Loch Ness monster.

The "Loch Ness monster" first appeared in 1871 when D McKenzie reported seeing a strange creature there – this is 1300 years later. The association with Loch Ness is primarily a Victorian invention. In addition the River Ness is 6 miles long, however it's catchment area includes all of the Rivers that flow into Loch Ness, these are

    River Ness
    River Farigaig
    River Enrick
    River Coiltie
    River Foyers
    River Fechlin
    Allt Breineag
    River E
    River Moriston

Allt Bhlaraidh
River Doe
River Loyne
Allt Doe
River Oich
River Garry
River Tarff

Columba's adventure could have taken place many, many miles from Inverness and in any river that may have flowed into Loch Ness, There is no guarantee that the Rivers that we know today had the same names in the dark ages.

- It depends entirely on it being the River Ness that we know today. Ne's is the Gaelic word for stoats and weasels. Would it be so surprising to see a "water beast" in a river populated with wildlife like stoats and weasels, and this description just makes the river any one of hundreds of rivers across Scotland.

- And of course the very last problem is that most of the tale regarding Columba's visit to Breide – his adventures around the River Ness and the curing of Briochan - is complete and utter nonsense. "Magic" pebbles, the ability to shout loud enough across water, over the sound of swimming shouting and screaming, and getting an untrained wild animal you have never seen before to obey you. Prophesies that have come true – i.e.,. fortune telling - that's the stuff of fairy tales, not the science of history.

It;s the final point that, unfortunately, highlights the problems we have with Adomnan's evidence (and that of later British historians e.g., Bede, Nennius etc.). How much is fact, how much is a "fairy tale", how much, whether deliberately or not, is accredited to the wrong person, how much is wishful thinking and how much is genuine. Their histories are written from uncorroborated stories, mixing fact with fiction, propaganda and nonsense.

Their approach was different to the earlier Roman writers, whose work contained a substantial amount of propaganda and bias, but with enough contemporary detail to work out the basics. The Roman approach was exaggerated and political to some extent but within the realms of acceptability, and a great deal can be deduced from it.

Adomnan's stories with ridiculous tales such as Columba's water beast, magic pebbles, prophesies and other such "miracles" by other saints and kings are a nonsense and greatly discredit it's value as a resource for the 6th century. Like Shakespeare, Adomnan wrote for an audience in his own time, interpolating the structure and political machinations of the 7th century into it. Adomnan was not writing a history book.

Bede

Bede is the author of most of our beliefs about the origins of the Picts, but, like Gildas, his history does not suggest that the Picts were indigenous either. According to Bede;

- They arrive in Ireland in a few warships from "Scythia", having been blown off course by unfavourable winds.

- They obtain wives from the Irish – namely Scots, and because of this they adopt a practice of matrilineal succession.

- The migrate from Ireland into the northern part of

Britain.

- They were (formerly) divided from the Britons by a large gulf of the sea, which runs far into the land and a strong city of the Britons stands there called Alcluith.

Like Gildas, Bede's account contradicts the view of the Picts as indigenous, but it also contradicts our view of the settlement of Britain. These are the 22nd, 23rd, 24th & 25th problems in our investigation;

- The Picts are not indigenous but come from Scandinavia.

- If they came from Scandinavia what winds could take them over the North Sea, completely missing out the entire North East Coast of Scotland, past the Orkneys, along the northern coast of Scotland, down past the Inner and Outer Hebrides. Then past the West Coast of Scotland, where they would surely have been able to see land, until they end up in the North of Ireland. It's not a realistic route to travel by either accident, or unfavourable winds.

- They are not an entire nation or a large number but only a few warships, filled with men, so any descendants are only a very, very small part "Pict".

- Bede mentions a large gulf of the sea which extends far into the land and separates the Britons of the south from the Picts, and then latterly the migrating Scots from Ireland. Alcluith, supposedly meaning "Rock of the Clyde" is then traditionally associated with Dumbarton Rock in the Clyde Estuary, however the River Clyde and Clyde estuary as shown below does not travel in the direction Bede suggests. It starts in the Southern Uplands, meandering northwards before flowing into the Firth of Clyde, as shown below

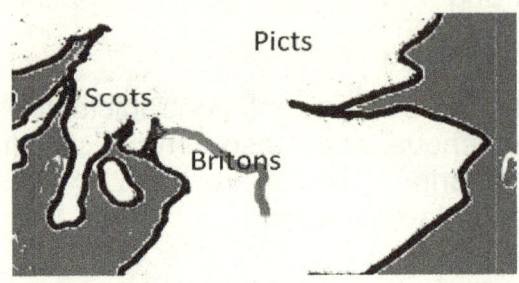

The Clyde therefore extends from the sea, down the middle of the land of "the Britons" and does not form a boundary between Britons and Scots or Britons and Picts. As can clearly be seen, Argyll, the traditional Scots homeland is part of the mainland and is not separated by any "Sea". Even Kintyre on the opposite side of the Firth of Clyde is a peninsula of the mainland and is accessible by a land route – there is no sea barrier between the people of Argyll, the Picts or the "Britons". According to Bede the Scots arrived on the North side of the Bay (of Alcluith), However Argyll, although directly North, is not situated across a Bay and the Kintyre peninsula where the Scots are thought to have originally settled lies directly west of the Clyde Estuary. In addition Dumbarton – traditionally thought to be Alcluith – is also on the North side of the Clyde Estuary. Bede's gulf of sea was definitely not the Clyde.

Only one Western Estuary divides North Britain from the South as Bede describes. The Solway Firth flows from the Irish Sea into a river basin area where it meets up with the River Nith and then the river Tweed, flowing into the North

Sea on the East Coast (this was the original Scottish-English Border in the early medieval period). The locations of the Scots, Picts and Britons can now be re-evaluated as shown in the following image.

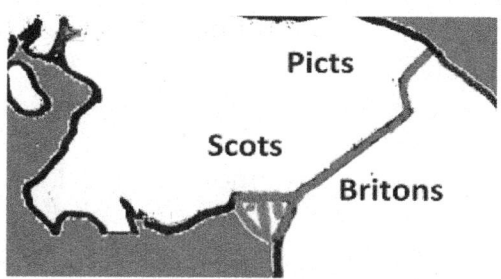

This is the area matching Bede's description, It ties in with the archaeology of Scotland, with evidence of Irish settlement in the South West, reaching as far as Perthshire, during the 6th century BC - 1st century AD. This matches the shape of Britain as it was believed to be up to the Tudor period. Bede's sources were secondary, being obtained in Rome by the presbyter Nothelm, and also Abbot Albinus of Canterbury. Ptolomey's Geographia was the main Roman source for World Geography and was used until late Medieval times, but Ptolomey had Scotland in the wrong orientation by almost 90 degrees, and we may wish to consider the impact this would have on the location of the "British" city of Alcluith, and the influence this may have had on other early map makers.

Chapter 2: Alcluith and The Early Maps

The 2nd century Greek geographer Ptolomey did not create a "map of the world" as such. There was no cartography involved, His work was literary based, a list of places, people and co-ordinates thought to have been obtained from earlier sources, travellers, sailors and soldiers that visited the known world. For Britain the co-ordinates had a significant error as the following illustration based on the 1493 Schedel-Munzer-Wolgemut Europa Map shows, but also including the Solway – Nith -Tweed link. This would have been the shape that Bede recognised as Britain.

(https://inter-antiquariaat.nl/antiek/oude-landkaarten-wereld/europa/neuremberg-chronicle)

The profile of Scotland and Northern England was rotated 90 degrees so the geography and dimensions are suspect. On the West coast the separation of Scotland from England starts below the Firth of Clyde, and not directly opposite or at the top of it. On the east coast the sea emerges from a river flowing almost continuously towards it from a "gulf" on the west – The only route that follows this path is the Tweed, which links with the Nith and the Solway. The Solway is created from the "gulf" occurring below the Firth of Clyde as shown below.

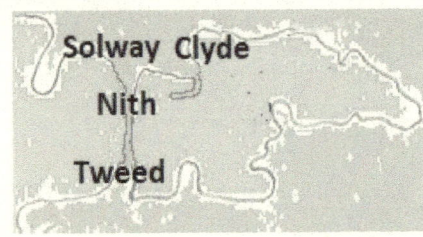

In Bede's history, the Picts travel from Ireland and took control of North Britain. The shortest route they could have taken was from Northern Ireland to the West Coast of Scotland, allowing them to take the Northern part of the country and subsequently being pushed eastwards (or north-eastwards) as the Scots migrate later. This border location on the Solway-Tweed would also tie in with the notion of Picts and Scots being "*overseas*" as Gildas claimed. One of the major problems with interpreting dark age tales is that of location and consideration whether place-names have remained static or whether they have been "moved". In the case of the "Clyde", there is very good evidence that it was "moved" in medieval times.

The first record of the Clyde appears to be in Ptolomey's Geographia, where it is listed as the Clota Estuary, it is placed on the northern coast above the Deucaledonius Ocean, along with other rivers and features

Novantarum peninsula – 21*00, Rerigonius bay – 20*30, Vindogara bay – 21*20, Clota estuary – 22*15, Lemannonius bay – 24*00. Epidium promontory – 23*00. mouth of the Longus river -24*30, mouth of the Itis river – 27*00. Volas bay – 29*00, mouth of the Navarus river – 30*00, Tarvedum or Orcas promontory -31*20
(http://penelope.uchicago.edu/Thayer/E/Gazetteer/Periods/Roman/_Texts/Ptolemy/2/2*.html#Vindogara_town)

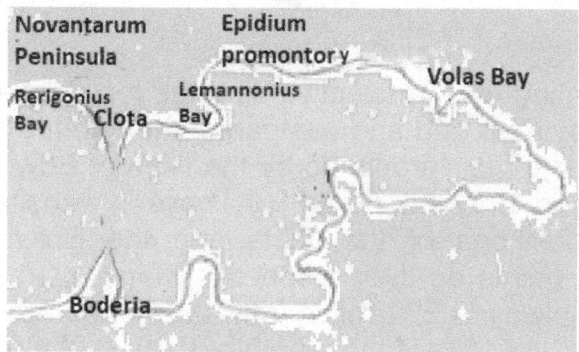

The Clota estuary was placed by Ptolomey in a different

location to the one we are familiar with for the Clyde. It is located below the Epidium promontory, further south than the Firth of Clyde. The river Clyde today is located in the North of the Firth of Clyde - the Clota and the river Clyde are in 2 different and opposite positions. The Clota appears to be the deepest inlet on the West Coast – It reaches further inland than any other estuary. On a modern map this would be the Solway, as can be seen in the following scaled images of Britain and the Ptolomeic map. The name Boderia on the Eastern side, may be related to the name Berwick, thought to be 10th century Anglo-Saxon, but with a 3rd/4th century Roman fort at Tweedmouth nearby.

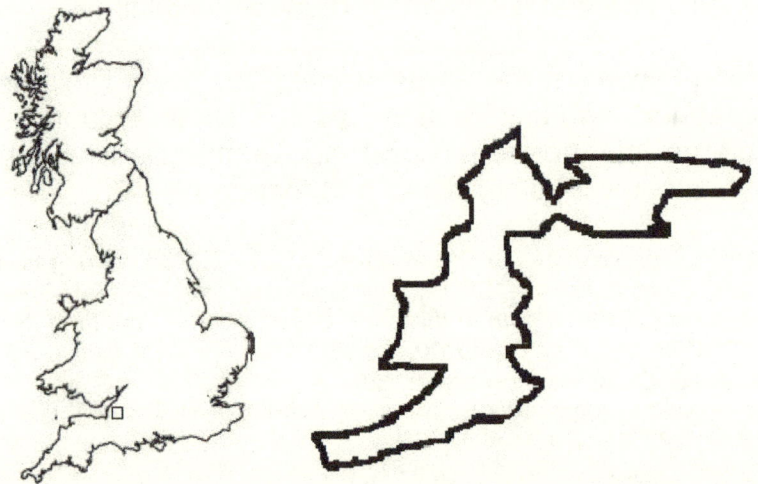

By calculating the respective lengths of Scotland on a modern day map and and comparing them to the version of the Ptolomeic map proposed by the likes of Edward Luther Stevenson in 1932 (found on Bill Thayer's website) we find that the positions of the Clota and the Solway are at equivalent points on their respective maps – On a modern map the Solway is 274 miles from the northernmost point– equating to 38.18% of the length of the UK. We find almost the same ratio on the Ptolomeic map – The Clota measures out to a position 37.77% of the length of Britain, making it likely that they were the same.

We can test this hypothesis further – By directly comparing scaled drawings of the Ptolomeic map against the profile of Britain, rotating the Ptolomeic map, by 90 degrees, until the North of Britain is in the correct orientation.

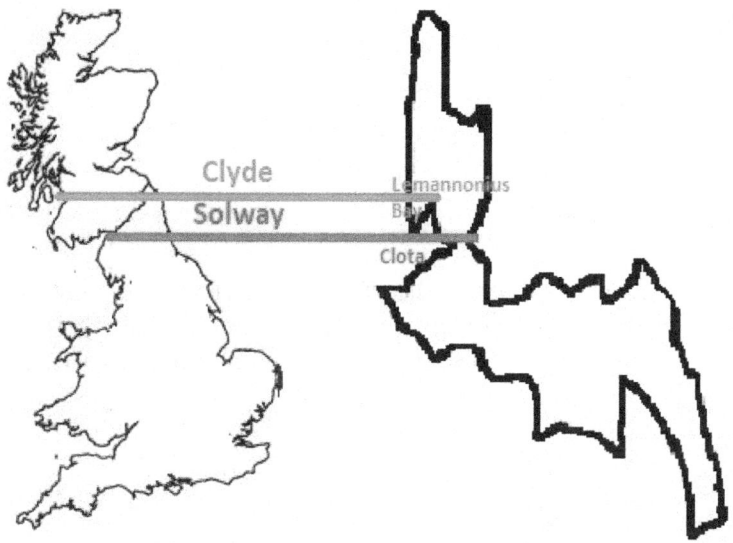

As can clearly be seen, the Solway lines up almost exactly with the Clota Estuary, the Firth of Clyde lines up with Lemannonius Bay. And the Epidium promontory is in a similar position on both maps as well.

Lemannonius Bay is in the Firth of Clyde that we know today., Although the Clyde/Clota estuary is named, the river Clyde itself was not significant enough to be recorded by Ptolomey – hardly surprising as it was in the Industrial age when it was widened and it, and the city of Glasgow, achieved real importance.

3 of the 6 cities of the Damnoni (or Dumnoni) – the

occupants of Strathclyde – Alauna, Lindum and Victoria are placed well above the Clyde estuary. The other 3 are situated just below it. As can be seen

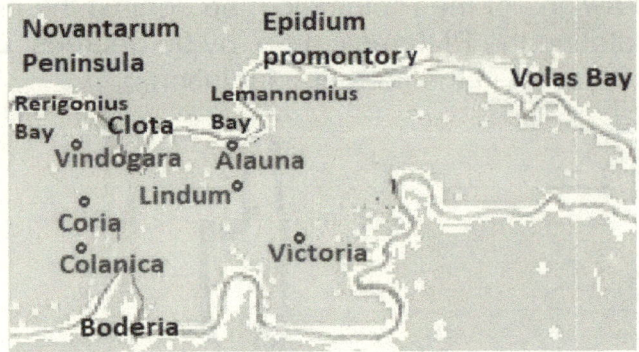

The territory of the Damnoni/Dumnoni is extensive, reaching from the Argyll to the Northern (Cumbrian) part of England. Bede says that the Scots settled North of the Bay – this does not necessarily mean that they remained just in that location.

Alcluith and Dumbarton

Identifying Alcluith is perhaps the biggest challenge we have faced. Traditionally Dumbarton is viewed as Alcluith, however Dumbarton dates from around the $5^{th}/6^{th}$ century AD. Bede indicates Alcluith was an important ancient site that was probably in existence from pre-Roman times, yet it is not in any of the names of "cities" named by Ptolomey. If it was in existence then it must have had a different name.

It is these name changes that present a problem – Alcluith must have had different name in the 2nd century AD and then between the 2nd century and the 8th century, it has become known as Alcluith, after this it experiences a further renaming and becomes Dunbritain and then Dumbarton, after the Scots took control of Strathclyde.

There is no supporting evidence that a practice of renaming towns was commonplace though. Most of the early settlements that we can find documents relating to, have retained names, or at least still contain part of the original name, that make them identifiable on ancient documents whether they are in the North or the South of Britain. The Scots did not rename Edinburgh, Glasgow, Perth, Scone etc. The association of Dumbarton to a "Fortress of Britons" relies entirely on the assumption that the word Dum is a corruption of the word Dun, which in itself is a shortened form of dun-cnuic, meaning hill fort. However this language corruption does not take place in other Northern territories – Dundee, Dunfermline, Dun Edin (Edinburgh) for example.

Dum appears in various Strathclyde territories, many of them dating from 4th, 5th and 6th centuries etc. The name Dum is by no means unique to Dumbarton – there is Dumfries, Dumbreck etc. Dum appears therefore to have a distinct meaning and we have to consider that the places it appears in were under the control of the **Dum**noni/ **Dam**noni. It seems far more likely that the word Dum originates from the name of the ancient tribe that occupied this region, in which case it is unlikely that the name has altered at all.

Early Maps

There are early maps of Scotland in existence, which were written at a time contemporary with the Scots supposed takeover of Strathclyde. One is the Anglo-Saxon map, written at Canterbury cathedral and dating from around 995 – 1050 AD. It is map of the world as it was known, including Britain. There is a strong indication in the names and places that it was contemporary with 10th century Britain. It would have taken several years to create so the map is likely to be using data from several years (probably decades) earlier.

https://upload.wikimedia.org/wikipedia/commons/f/f0/Cotton_world_map.jpg

There is only one division separating the North (Scotland) from the south and the line is clearly drawn at the Solway-Tweed region. I disagree with the current evaluation of the the name in North Britain being camri. This section has suffered badly from diistortion and wear, however we can clearly see the faint impression of a S (highlighted below) at the start of the word followed by a small c, then an o, t and s.

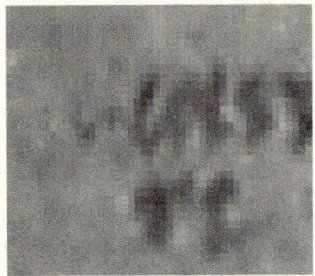
Section with faint S

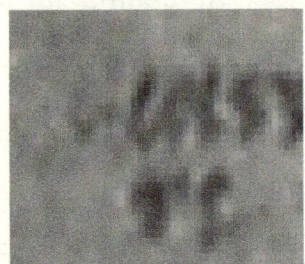
Highlighted faint S

The last letter after the s may be an A. The phrase may simply intend to say Scots Are or Ari - (Are deriving from the Latin word area). We can see this by simply rearranging the letters – taking a S from another section and blending it with the impression where the intial S belongs and moving the A in front of the re

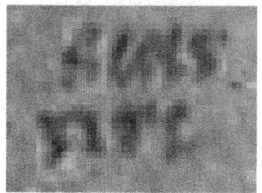

I think it's highly unlikely but it's possible that the S may be due to other environmental factors, but we see the same shape of c, o, t and s in other sections of the map. I have shown these below;

c   o   t   s

The first 5 letters were definitely to be read as Scots

The map exhibits evidence of a 10th century nomenclature for places so it suggests the creators were using 10th century rather than 11th century data. This map indicates that Scots were inhabiting Southern Scotland well before the battle of Carham in 1018AD, when they allied with Malcolm III against Uchtred of Northumbria.

Ireland is clearly in the wrong orientation with the north of Ireland being placed directly opposite the Solway. This is an important feature as it means that it was believed that the most direct route from Antrim, the ancient homeland of the Scots, to Britain was across the Irish sea to the Solway.

Little appears to be known of the geography or placenames in the North of Scotland, and this too is important in assessing the earlier work of Bede. This document was produced in Canterbury and it was an early Canterburian monk, Abbot Albinus from St Augustine's Abbey, that helped provide Bede with his source material, so it is likely that this would limit the information Bede had access to. Bede's work was already well know by the 11th century and with the lack of detail shown here, we can assume that the producers of this map were limiting the words of Bede, relating to Scots, Picts and Britons, to the areas distinctly shown – Southern Scotland below the Firth of Clyde. This would mean that to the Anglo-Saxons, the Firth of Clyde and further North has little, if any relevance or importance, so for Alcluith to have the importance it holds for Bede, it would have to have been located farther South.

Essentially this map proves that the Scots were present in the South of Scotland from a much earlier period than currently accepted. It is also likely to have fed into the creation of another early map, known as the Hereford Mappi Mundi, written c. 1300 AD.

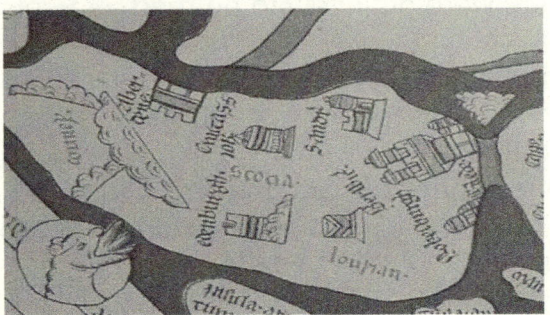

(https://upload.wikimedia.org/wikipedia/commons/1/1b/Hereford_Mappa_Mundi_detail_Britain.jpg)

This is an important time in Scottish history as it was created around the time of the Wars of Independence, when the English King Edward was claiming overlordship of Scotland. If there had been any suggestion that Scotland, or the Scots had "usurped" another kingdom or renamed an ancient capital, it would have been mentioned on this document to use as a political tool to help establish

Edward's right of overlordshp of Britain. This may be the reason for naming the region of Lothian and Couney (Caithness & Sutherland) separately but the western towns Sanor (Sanquhar) and what appears to be a unusual representation of Glasgow – *Chlitassjoh* - a combination of Clyde and Glasgow. Clearly the "ancient" name Strathclyde had no significance in Scotland in the 13th century.

The places that are mentioned on the Hereford map must be considered the most prominent administrative towns/cities of 13th century Scotland. These are Aberdeen, Edinburgh, Berwick, Sanquhar (Sanor), Glasgow, Roxburgh and Melrose. The names Dumbarton or Alcluith or any variants do not appear. This map provides early evidence of a Gaelic Strathclyde – Saquhar is a Gaelic name, so the first Gaelic placename we find in the map is in the South West of Scotland and much farther south than Dumbarton.

There is also no distinct Argyll district, Pictavia, Scone, Dunadd, or Inverness. These held no importance to the individuals creating this map. Like the 11th century Anglo-Saxon map, the Clyde and the Firth of Clyde is not mentioned and has little if any importance. There is only one important estuary in the Scottish region – The Solway.

Other Maps

Dumbarton does not appear to be included on the most extensive of Matthew Paris' maps c.1250AD. The closest name is Dunbrain, but this is in completely the wrong place – North of Stirling and being situated on a river going from south to north.

https://upload.wikimedia.org/wikipedia/commons/4/44/Britannienkarte_des_Matthew_Paris.jpg

He does however, mention Glasgow (Glascu) but unlike other rivers on the map, not the name of the Clyde. He writes fluvius factes Cludesdale – *the river became Clydesdale* and appears to put a year of 1208 next to it.

In another Matthew Paris map – a far more basic version - we do see the first record of Glasgow and the Clyde.

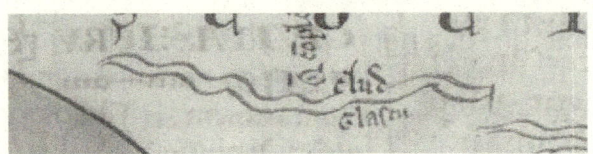

http://www.medievalhistories.com/wp-content/uploads/Royal-14-C-vii-fol-5v-M-Paris-map-Britain-crop.jpg

In this map though, while the Clyde does appear to be called clud, it is not seen as extending to the sea and again Dumbarton is not mentioned. Glasgow was founded on a ford, where the confluence of the Molendinar burn and the Clyde was at it shallowest. The word clud or cluith means "carrier" and with it being written directly above Glascu (Glasgow), on the top line of the river symbol probably relates to the movement of goods and people across the ford. These maps indicate that the river Clyde does not have an ancient name, the name arose (c.1208) when the district of Clydesdale was established, and the district took it's name from the use of the ancient ford at Glasgow.

The River Clyde and Dumbarton both appear together in the Gough Map of c.1360, although there is evidence of later medieval amendments. The addition of Dumbarton may be one of the these amendments but this is the first time we see a physical representation of a "fort" or castle building on a map relating to it.

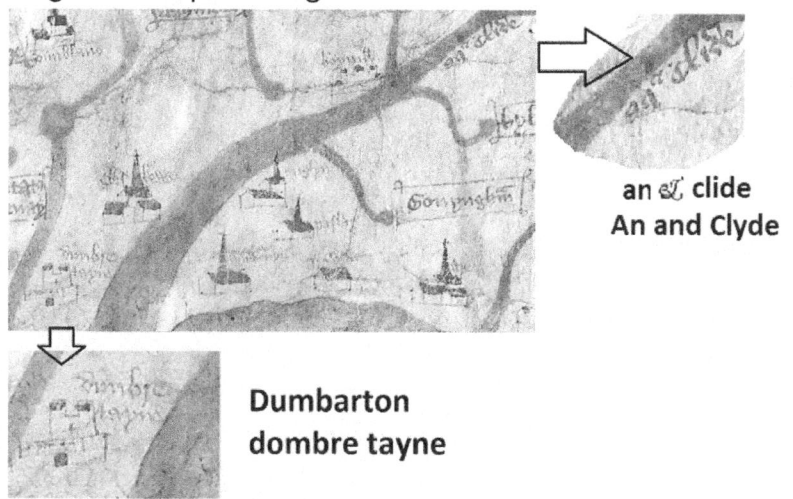

an & clide
An and Clyde

Dumbarton
dombre tayne

https://en.wikipedia.org/wiki/Gough_Map#/media/File:Gough_Kaart_(hoge_resolutie).jpg
(Dumbarton is in the botttom left hand corner, an & clide is in the top right hand corner)

The name Clide appears some distance from Dumbarton – almost at the river's source. It appears in the text *an & clide* with the Latin ampersand symbol. Glasgow does not appear on the map, but this text appears in it's place, just after the point where 2 rivers have converged into one – these would be the Molendinar and the Clyde. An is likely to be a variant of the word Aln - the same name as a number of rivers throughout Britain - and may just mean a river as it has an Indo-European origin relating to a flow or stream. The word an precedes the clide, and with the clud written opposite Glasgow in Matthew Paris' earlier map, it appears the name of the river Clyde was originally An. Clide refers to the crossing point on the river, an & clide means *"river and crossing"*. The clide was used to carry goods across the river – it was the point at which the river could be crossed.

Dumbarton's earliest appearance on a map is therefore c. 1360 almost the same name we know it as today. Dombre tayne, with the Dum part of the name at the start, and ending with the Gaelic word tayne, meaning spoil, plunder, cattle etc. which is linked to the modern word town.

The next time we see Dumbarton, it still does not appear as Dun briton or a variant. It is in John Harding's mid 15th century map. In this map the river that flows past it (and Glasgow) is an extension of the River Forth flowing from the East Coast towards the West. This river does not reach the Firth of Clyde. It is yet another Map where the Clyde has no name or significance and Dumbarton is clearly named as Dubretayn as shown – (the same tayn ending as before).

https://www.bl.uk/picturing-places/articles/medieval-maps-of-regions

As the centuries wore on, many maps started to appear, the Regno de Scota (c 1558) which has no name for the river that Glasgow sits on, the 1572 map by Thomaso Porcacchi, where we find Cuasco (Glasgow), on the river Clauda, and Dombreton (Dumbarton) completely out of place - much further north, nowhere near the river. In the 1573 Scotia Tabula map we find that the name of the Firth of Clyde was the Dunbreton Fyrth – the first Dunbarton, "fortress of britons", nearly 800 years after Bede's Alcluith, and 200 years after dombretayne appeared on the Gough map.

In summary, during the 11th century Dumbarton was located in a site that there was little, or no, knowledge of in the Anglo-Saxon world. It was north of the route that the Anglo-Saxons believed the Irish had taken, from Antrim towards the Solway, to occupy Scotland. It only starts to appear on maps around the mid 14th century onwards and the indications are that it was an important Scots, rather than British, settlement, there is no evidence that it had any name relating to a hill fort or Dun prior to the late medieval period.

The Clyde's first appearance was opposite Glasgow (not Dumbarton) and it related to the point where the river could be crossed over, As Glasgow grew in importance during the early medieval period, this crossing became associated with the district and then the river. The rivers' original name was a version of the fairly common Aln, changing to the Clyde sometime between the 13th - 15th century.

There is really only one conclusion. The maps from the 11th - 14th century demonstrate that Dumbarton and Alcluith are 2 distinct and unrelated places. Alcluith could not have been named for the Clyde and Dumbarton is likely to take part of it's name from the ancient tribe that was resident in this area – the **Dum**noni/**Dam**noni.

With the archaeological evidence proving that Scots from Ireland settled in the Solway – Clyde region, we can speculate that the statement on the 8th century Senchus Fer n' Alban that Fergus Mor Mac Erc held a part of Britain, actually meant that Fergus Mor Mac Erc seized or rather established Dum Barton, and this would agree with the evidence of the fortress on Dumbarton rock being constructed around the 5th/6th century AD.

Association of Dumbarton and Alcluith

The association with the Clyde and Alcluith probably became fixed around the late 16th and early 17th century with 3 maps. The first being Abraham Ortelius' map of 1573 when he writes *Cloyd flu olim Alcluth. He* calls Dumbarton, Duuberton – no link to a Dun, or "fortress" yet. In a 1578 map, Bishop Leslie altered the name to Donbriton, but did not name the Firth, or the river Clyde, or refer to Alcluith, but in this map Bishop Leslie placed the Novantum Promontory in the Kintyre region.

https://maps.nls.uk/view/00000258

Bishop Leslie may have believed that Dumbarton was the "Fort of the Britons" but he also believed the location of the "fort" was related to the position of Ptolomey's Novantarum promontory, which was actually located below the Clota estuary. Whether the Clyde was the Solway or not, the Novantum promontory on this map was incorrect and therefore so was Leslie's "Donbriton".

It was in Mercator's 1595 map of Southern Scotland, and the following section that the association was fixed.

https://maps.nls.uk/scotland/rec/131

An apparent link between the 1573 and 1578 maps placing the Clyde, Dumbarton and Alcluith together, but it took almost 800 years for this association to appear. On this map Dumbarton is called Dunbritoun, but this leads to more problems. Toun is a very basic form of town – Dun britoun would be Hiill-fort of Bri town, not the fort of the Britons. The phrase written along the Clyde is often translated as *Clyde once known as Alcluith*, but if so, it is incorrectly phrased, it would have been *Quae Clyde cum Alcluith.*

He may have meant the *Clyde river once Alcluth,* but the meaning is unclear, The river was never called Alcluith. According fo Bede the "city" was Alcluith, the river was Cluith, while we know that our river Clyde was probably called the Aln originally, and can therefore only date the use of the name Clyde as a relatively recent change, that occurred during the 13th century. Also Mercator clearly writes Aleluth - an e rather than a c, Ortelius used the name Duubreton and Bishop Leslie had the Novantum promontory too far north.

It was in 1607 that William Hole finally linked the Clota of Ptolomey to the Firth of Clyde, or rather the Fyrth of Dunbrytan.

https://maps.nls.uk/view/00000200

None of his predecessors had gone so far as to name the Clota of Ptolomey as the Firth of Dumbarton, and in doing so William Hole, like Bishop Leslie, placed it in completely the wrong place – entirely opposite to the position Ptolomey used - and left a conundrum, He gave 2 names for the same stretch of water, using a variant of the ancient name Clota for the Estuary and then used the modern name

Clyde for the River.

In 1610 John Speed produced his Map of the Kingdome of Scotland, and William Hole's Glotta Aesterium was not included, the Firth of Clyde was back to it's original name being named the Firth of Dumbrytton.

The combination of the Ortelius' Cloyd flu olim Alcluth, Donbriton of Bishop Leslie, Aleluth of Mercator's 1595 map and the Glotta Aesterium of William Hole's 1607 map linked the Alcluith of Bede to Dumbarton but the evidence suggests otherwise. The association between Dumbarton and Alcluith gained ground in the late Tudor and Stuart period, and this is the period in which there was a political desire amongst some (not all) influential people in both Scotland and England to unite the 2 separate kingdoms under one protestant monarch. The Stewarts had long held ambitions in England – Margaret Tudor, the daughter of Henry VII had married James IV in 1503. The Tudors were of Welsh origin and Henry VII used the red dragon of Wales as a symbol to gather supporters in Wales during the Wars of the Roses. His son, Henry VIII, used the Welsh dragon as an emblem on Royal Navy ships. Having a connection to a "Welsh" kingdom in Scotland would be beneficial to Stewart ambitions. Also demonstrating, whenever possible that it was an evolutionary process for smaller kingdoms to merge together may also have been seen as advantageous – particularly in Scotland, where some reassurance may have been needed that a Scots king taking over a large neighbouring kingdom, would not necessarily lead to the demise of the smaller kingdom.

The meaning of Alcluith

It may be possible that there has been some confusion between Ptolomey's Alauna and Dumbarton. Alauna, one of a number of places throughout Britain with the same name, was in Strathclyde on the banks of the Firth of Clyde according to Ptolomey. This location though appears to relate to the Roman harbour, whose archaeological remains were found, relatively recently, near Hunterston in North Ayrshire. Nearby is the Avondale Roman road where goods and people could be transported to and from the harbour. This location is farther South than Dumbarton and several miles from the River Clyde. Cluith was unlikely to relate to the Firth of Clyde, as Bede calls the cluith a river rather than an estuary and the Firth of Clyde, was known as the Firth of Dumbarton or Dunbrytton until relatively recently.

It is also unlikely that this Alauna was in existence in Bede's lifetime the Roman Army had retreated back to the line of Hadrian's Wall in the 3rd century AD abandoning a number of sites in the process. In Ravenna's Cosmographia of the 8th century it does not appear at all, indicating that it was no longer in use. There does not appear to be any relationship between Alcluith, Alauna (of Strathclyde) and Dumbarton..

Our view of Dark Age history is inconsistent on a number of important points. From Ptolomey's map, the Novantae and the Selgovae would both be located below the Solway-Tweed line in the Cumbrian region. Alcluith would not be the hill fort on Dumbarton Rock as it does not tie in with Bede's description, of a surviving, possibly thriving, pre-roman settlement, still in existence in his day. The hill fort on Dumbarton Rock, constructed in the 5th/6th century would have been one of the youngest settlements in post Roman Britain.

We have to consider the likelihood that Alcluith was not in Strathclyde at all. Dumbarton did not exist until the 5th/6th century, Alauna had been abandoned and the Roman Army had retreated back from the Antonine Wall to the Hadrian's wall border in the 3rd century AD. With the disruption and instability present in Strathclyde during the Roman period, is it really likely that a major British city would survive, or that the Roman Army would let it survive, when there is evidence of continuing resistance and rebellion to Roman rule by the local inhabitants?.

There may be a clue to Alcluith's location in the name. There is an anomaly in the translation, assumed to be a welsh term meaning "Rock of the Clyde". The word cluith commonly associated with the word Clud or Clyde, means transportation, and the variant cluit means carrier or transporter, Alcluith therefore does not automatically link to the name of the Clyde. The word Al, or as it also appears in some sources, Alt, does not exist in Welsh. The welsh word for Rock is Rock, and for an island it is Ynys. It does, however exist in Gaelic, where it signifies a method, way or route. The name Alcluith therefore would relate to a city that developed along a transportation route – it was a trading centre.

"Rock of the Clyde"

Bede refers to Alcluith being "Rock Cluith" because it was situated near the river of that name. Cluith indicates a transportation method so has Bede been misinterpreted The latin for rock can be *moles, mons, scopules, cautes* or *rupis* but Bede choses to use another word *petram* instead, and unlike Cluith it does not begin with a capital letter, the phrase is *petram Cluith*. Petra is the part which infers a rock or a stone, but the word petram indicates an inflection of stone/rock, i.e. petram Cluith could signify a place where the direction changes towards/away from "Cluith" on a stone/rocky surface. Like the word cluith, it also appears to be directional relating to movement.

Bede's Rock of the Clyde was, in fact, a reference to a site built around/on an inflecting stony/rocky landscape, which was used as a route for transportation, trade and settlement. The likeliest place for this site would be the Solway Firth. Solway is a name that arose around the 12th century, it is a Norse name that came from the Viking settlement of the 10th century and can be placed no earlier than that. We therefore do not know what the name of the Solway was prior to the 10th century, however there is clue in the name, the *way* part originates from the Scandinavian word *wath* meaning to wade/ford, this could link it to the word Al and cluith as both relate to a route or way across a river.

The Irish sea flows into the Solway Firth, which in turn, flows to the river Nith, (containing the latter *ith* element of the word *cluith*), and would provide a direct trading route between Ireland and the West coast of Britain, thus trade and settlement can occur in both directions. This would be an established route for Irish setters to use in occupying the West Coast of Northern Britain. Archaeological evidence from the Solway region shows Irish settlement occurred here between the 6th century BC and the 1st century AD.

We can even speculate that the phrase Bede used has been entirely misinterpreted. The literal translation is

"the city of Alcluith, which in their language signifies the inflection of stone, Cluith is by the river of that name"

Bede doesn't specifically say that it is by the river Cluith or Clyde – he says *by the river of that name*. The phrase he uses is *nominis illus* – nominis is latin for name. Bede could just have meant that the river was named illus, which, if you remove the latin us ending, tells us that Alcluith was situated by a river named "ill". There is one stand out candidate for a river named ill, that flows into the Solway Firth from the Cumbrian region – the River Ellen.

Another Alauna & Alcluith

The River Ellen is a variant of the word Aln, the name of several rivers in Britain - the River Allan in Central Scotland, The Ale water in Berwickshire, that was formerly known as the Aln, the River Aln in Northumberland etc. It is likely that the settlements of Alauna derived their name from the local river, hence there are several Alaunas listed by Ptolomey as there are several rivers called Aln.. We can see that the names of many settlements around these rivers still contain the Aln part of the name – but almost always at the start of the name – Ellenfoot, Alnwick, Alnmouth. etc. Alcluith, contrary to the accepted translation of Bede's statement, referred to a place named after the local river, a version of Aln near the Cluith.

One place fits this description and can be dated to the first century AD, when the Roman Fort in this area played an important strategic role in protecting the Romano-British territories from invasion from the North. This is Maryport, a harbour town that can be dated to the 1st century AD, in the Allerdale region of Cumbria. Prior to 1749, it's name was Ellenfoot and this means it was named after the River it was close to, as Bede claimed. It was also known by a different name during the Roman period - Alauna (one of a number of different Alauna's in Britain).

The "Rock", petram, may simply be a metaphorical phrase representing the fortifications and their peninsular location. The 1st century AD Roman Fort was built 40 meters above sea level on a sandstone ridge and the later fort, built c 122 AD, formed part of the Hadrian's Wall defences. There was a flourishing Roman harbour and a large civilian settlement.

From it's location the Solway Firth and the Northern region could be monitored for incoming and outgoing travellers, trade and possible threats from hostile tribes, and maintain a relatively stable existence. Maryport is by far the likeliest candidate for Alcluith. We can even speculate that there is an error in copying – the word petram is similar to the word portum which means harbour – petram Cluith may be be portum Cluith. Bede's phrase would be

"the city of Alcluith, which in their language signifies the harbour of Cluith, is by the river named illus"

which simply means;

"the city of Alcluith, which in their language signifies the harbour of Cluith, is by the river named Ellen"

In other words Alcluith, meaning the harbour of the Clota [Solway] is by the River Ellen, which it is named after. Matthew Paris's 13th century map shows a Cumbrian clud.

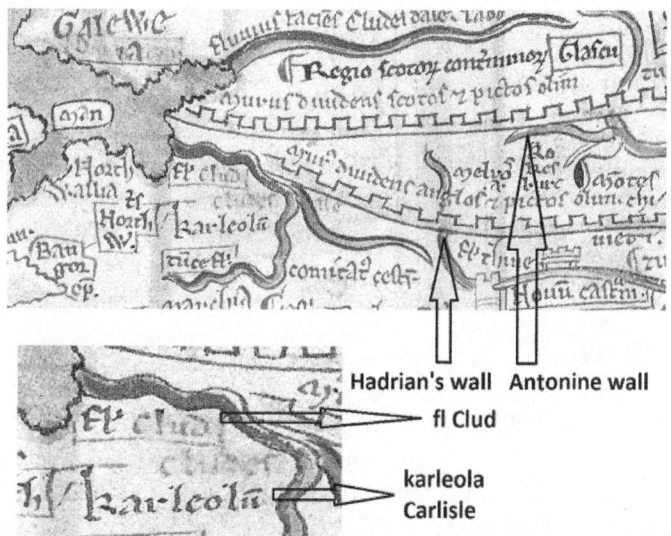

Hadrian's wall   Antonine wall
fl Clud
karleola
Carlisle

https://upload.wikimedia.org/wikipedia/commons/4/44/Britannienkarte_des_Matthew_Paris.jpg

We can see from this is not the same Clud or Clyde that

Matthew Paris placed opposite Glasgow. This second clud is sited in Cumbria, below Galloway and runs through Cheviotdale to the Solway firth, at the end of Hadrian's Wall, exactly where we expect it to be. This appears to confirm that the term cluith or clud was a feature on the river rather than it's name. Some may even have mistaken it as Alclud, but it was in fact fl clud – fl being short for fluvius, meaning a river. Like the ford that Glasgow was built on, clud indicates a river crossing. A Cumbrian "Clyde" in the Solway firth below Hadrian's wall. In fact we can go even further, there were multiple Alauna's, there were probably multiple cluds as well – it had nothing to with a river name – After all Bede uses the term "signifies". Alcluith was a harbour with a river crossing, the point where the harbour of a city "named" Alauna flows to or from the sea, where boats and people can transport goods to many different directions and Bede's phrase just means;

"the city of Alcluith, which in their language signifies the harbour crossing, is by the river named Ellen"

After the Roman Army left, Maryport's significance gradually declined, but the remnants of the Roman architecture and buildings were still visible up to the 18th century. We know that Alauna/Maryport/Ellenfoot was in existence, and still a significant site, while Bede was alive. It is named in Ravenna's Cosmographia, written around 732AD, and contemporary with Bede.

Considerations

Bede and Ptolomey are 2 of the key sources we use for studying British Dark Age history, however we have to consider the errors in their work in order to find out how reliable their details are, and both show significant issues that we have to compensate for;

Ptolomey's map

To create the shape of Britain, the northern half was rotated by 90 degrees. To retain the correct length of approximately 800 miles, Ptolomey had to "bend" the island, the area underneath the "bend" would have to overlap significantly with other territories, or else be "concertinaed" - (i.e. the shape an accordion creates when both sides are pushed together), This is illustrated below where I have used a simple triangle shape to represent Britain. This shape was chosen deliberately as this was the description of Britain used by the Roman Geographer Diodorus Siculus around 56BC. In the illustration, the red area shows the area of overlap when the top 1/3 of the triangle is rotated.

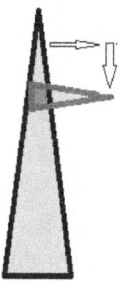

Ptolomey would have had to reduce the Northern region by at least 700 square miles to create the shape and retain the same length of approx 800 miles. This would have the effect of reducing the total length of the visible eastern side while leaving the visible western side at the correct length. So we can conclude that the shape created by Ptolomey is the result of him "bending" Britain in the same way. Ptolomey appears to have miscalculated his co-ordinates and has had to amend the dimensions of Britain to fit.

We can compensate for Ptolomey's miscalculations and draw the map in the way it should have appeared. We can find the corresponding trajectories, angles and separate and rotate the Northern section. Repositioning it against the Southern section and join them together in the correct alignment as shown on he following diagram..

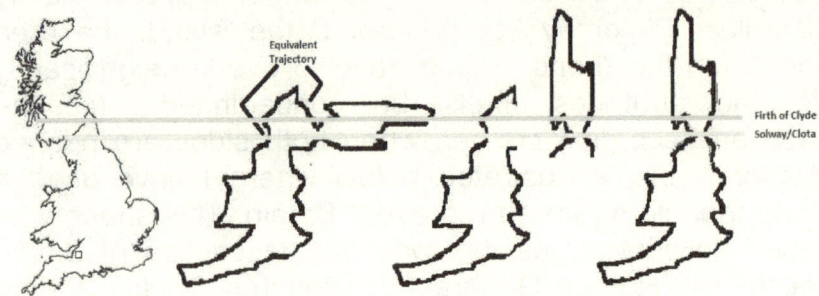

This is something that we can easily recognise as a representation of Britain. The points to note are clear enough the Clota remains in exactly the same alignment as the Solway Firth, The Firth of Clyde remains in the same position. The Clota and the Firth of Clyde are clearly separate features. Indeed we could speculate that as the islands within the Firth of Clyde are not recorded, they have been recorded as part of the mainland i.e. in the Lemannonius Bay area. Lemannonius Bay, has an obvious similarity in the initial part of the name to Lamlash – a town located near the southern tip of the largest island in the Firth of Clyde, Arran. But this new shape leaves us with a problem regarding the location of the Novantae and the Selgovae. It places them as occupying the region below the river Nith – not far below and well above Hadrian's wall.

We still have some features to account for - two missing features – Galloway - the promontory between the Clyde and the Solway and, as discussed earlier, the Tweed and the Forth which appears to have been combined into one.

The Clyde and the Solway are in the correct alignment as they were on the West Side, but the Firth of Forth on the

East side has been moved down and merged with the Tweed. We can correct that by adjusting the map, from the point at which the map was rotated – the Clota. When we "rotated" the North of Britain to the correct location we should have compensated for the areas that merged together – in the Novantarum peninsula – The Clota would have moved underneath this while the South East Coastline would have moved upwards. By doing this we can unmerge the overlapping, concertinaed area, selecting and placing the elements that were missing back into the correct position as shown;

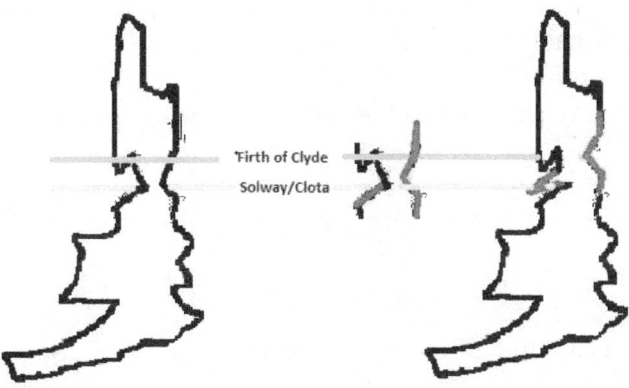

This means that the territories and tribes of the Novantae and Selgovae that were underneath the Clota have moved further North, placing them in the Border Region between Scotland and England – exactly where they were thought to be, and where we would expect them, particularly with local placenames such as Nithsdale, Selkirk etc. indicating a connection with them, but with the bonus that we now have a recognisable map of Britain.

The Clota remains the Solway, Lemannonius Bay remains in the Firth of Clyde, we have the Firth of Forth and Galloway. We haven't created a new promontory on Ptolomey's map though. The promontory was already there

– as the following diagram taken from an exploded view of the 1493 Schedel-Munzer-Wolgemut Map shows.

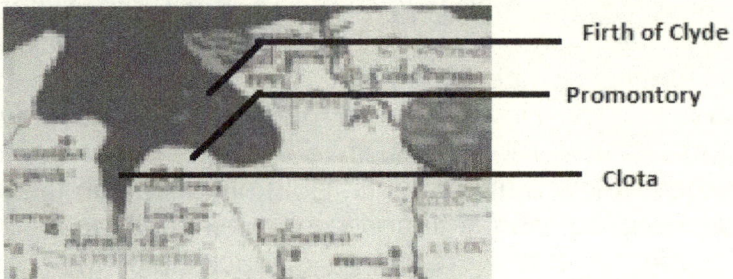

All we have really done is expand this smaller promontory feature, reflecting a correction in it's size and location due to the inaccuracies in Ptolomey's calculations. We can even see the similarity in the profile of the Clota estuary to the Solway if we were to rotate this section by 90 degrees.

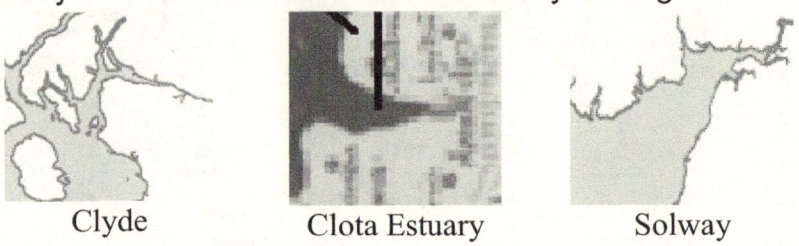

Clyde   Clota Estuary   Solway

It is very clearly closer in shape to the Solway than the Clyde, which has a down facing V shape travelling towards the southern uplands. The Clota and the Solway have slightly upward trajectories, travelling northwards to the river Nith, and eventually the Tweed.

We can work out exactly what went wrong with Ptolomey's original calculations. It is often assumed that it was because he used many different sources, but this is normal practice in the modern environment - gather as much evidence from as many different reliable sources as possible. This allows cross referencing and the correction of errors to take place. This didn't happen with Ptolomey – he retained crucial errors which were not corrected. He was not able to cross reference – so there could only have been one source for each set of co-ordinates he used.

We can reasonably guess who provided these co-ordinates. We can rule out the use of it being for sea navigation as there are too many errors. The "map" is a series of straight line co-ordinates missing several important features, not least of which is the entire section of the Galloway, the islands of the Firth of Clyde - and the various natural harbours and inlets that a sailor would need to know to identify safe havens, allow for tidal currents, rocks and islands and other hazardous features. They would not be able to use the information Ptolomey provided.

The other possible use would be military, maps were extremely valuable and very expensive due to the advantages they provided in war, identifying sites of strategic importance, identifying distances between them, travelling routes, roads to travel, areas for shelter and the location of allies and enemies - this was the likeliest use. Rome was a military power, it's solders were very industrious engineers, laying out fortifications and roads that lasted hundreds of years. To do this they needed to plot points and map out the most direct routes for their military purposes, hence the affinity for building straight roads. It was from these soldiers that Ptolomey would have obtained his information. Measurements would have been taken, as Roman Army progressed through the land. It would have been a stage by stage approach. They could not have used one datum point, it would have changed as they progressed. The end point of one stage would have been the start point of the next. The disadvantages of this approach are many, If a stage is missed out or lost it is not included, inaccuracies in one measurement would carry through to the next and could subsequently multiply.

Ptolomey's map was from a source not intended to outline the profile of a country – It was a route map. It was laying down the co-ordinates to reach a specific point as quickly as possible. Over the course of hundreds of miles and hundreds of co-ordinates being recorded, the risk of error and mistaking one reference point for another was great.

Also as a route map it reflected the Roman Army's progression through the land, rather than the shape of the island. It would include any deviations that they took – including retreats, advances, criss crosses and different directions when they encountered some insurmountable obstacles, mountains, rivers, and violent opposition on their journey. The Army's movements would show unusual patterns.

Ptolomey's work demonstrates that such errors and unusual movement occurred – The co-ordinates he gained access to gave the impression that the land on one edge was longer than the land on the other edge. The image below shows what needed to be done - one left sided "coastline" of 3 sections, and one 2 section right sided "coastline".

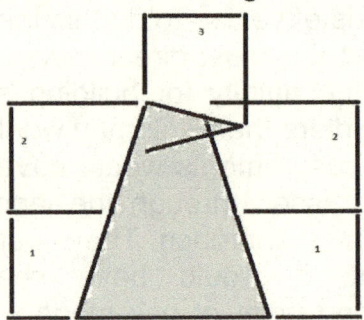

The short side in Ptolomey's map is the Eastern coastline of Scotland, This is where the biggest error took place. A measurement between stages in the East has been "missed" making the length of land in the East shorter than the West, and we know where this took place. The Forth

Estuary appears in the place where the Tweed should be but this was next to the name Boderia – Ptolomey has linked the Tweed and Forth together. It was the stage between Berwick and Edinburgh that went "missing". The map is bent because someone "misplaced" the co-ordinates for the stage between Berwick and Edinburgh.

When Ptolomey "Bent" the land, the gap where the Clota appeared had to widen significantly, because the effect was the same as happens when a fragile object is bent at a point - there is a fracture and the fracture opens wider as the bending increases. This is why the shape is the way it is with the Clota reaching so far inland, and a very small promontory preceding it, With only one continuous land mass visible looking south from the Epidium promontory, the assumption is that the Novantarum peninsula was part of the Cumbrian region rather than a separate feature.

This however is not unusual – the Galloway peninsula shape is missing from the 11th century Anglo-Saxon Map, Matthew Paris' 1250 map, the 13th century Mappi Mundi, and the 14th century Gough Map. It was not until the late Tudor/early Stuart period that we got close to a recognisable shape of this particular peninsula, by which time most of the early sources had already completed their work on the Dark Ages.

Later additions and amendments to Bede's work

Bede's work also has to be taken in the context that his personal knowledge and experience was very limited. If his biography is to be believed, almost his entire life was spent in a monastic order in Northumbria, with little direct contact with the secular world outside. Most of his information was second hand at best. Another problem lies with it's authenticity. The original version of Bede's work does not

exist and the versions we use are based on several different medieval copies with significant differences between them. Some writers assert that the first section – that contains the origins of the Britons, the Picts and the Scots has been inserted much later and is not genuine.
(http://www.electricscotland.com/history/early4-1.htm)

If this is the case then the testimonies of Bede, Nennius etc regarding the Scots origins can be completely ignored, as we would do with any evidence from uncorroborated and unreliable sources. Our only genuine evidence for Irish settlement in Scotland is with the archaeology, and the archaeology confirms Irish settlement was from the Solway region up to Perthshire between the 6th century BC and the 1st century AD and no later than this.

The Dumnoni of Strathclyde

The paradox of Scottish history is that the Irish links to the Dumnoni/Damnoni of Strathclyde are generally accepted. They appear to be related to the semi-mythical Fir Domnaan, named in the Lebor Gabala Erinn and settled in the Leinster/Mayo regions. This document was translated by TF O'Rahhilly and he concluded that the Fir Domnaan were part of a P-Celtic Brythonic settlement, subsequently superseded by Gaelic settlers. This reinforced the notion of the "Irish" origins of the Dumnoni as Brythonic. However the notion of a "Brythonic Irish" period has now been dismissed by modern scholars. The Irish territories attributed to this people were Gaelic speaking long before the 1st century AD, yet this "update" to a Gaelic Fir Domnaan has not led to a revision of the "ethnicity" of the Strathclyde Dumnoni. A Gaelic Fir Domnaan should have meant a Gaelic Dumnoni who came in via Antrim and the Tracht Romha – *the way ahead* (the Irish name for the Solway). There is no doubt that Romha is a word connected with both Riata and Rueda, the legendary Irish leader of the emigrant Scots.

Chapter 3 : The Pictish King List

At present there is only one Ptolomeic tribe that can be tied to the Picts. Yet the early medieval sources may provide more information. The Picts disappear around the beginning of the 10th century, but there is one document from around this time that we find produced in a "Pictish area" and that purports to be the list of kings going back to Cruithne "The Great Judge". And it is in the sequence of Brudes that appear in this "genealogy" that we find the names of other Pictish tribes

The 30 Brudes

Traditionally known as the 30 Brudes, this sequence contains only 28 names, which can be arranged as follows

Brude Pant	Brude Urpant
Brude Leo	Brude Urleo
Brude Gant	Brude Urgant
Brude Gnith	Brude Urgnith
Brude Fecir	Brude Urfecir
Brude Cal	Brude Urcal
Brude Cint	Brude Urcint
Brude Fec	Brude Urfec
Brude Ru	Brude Urru
Brude Gart	Brude Urgart
Brude Cinid	Brude Urcinid
Brude Uip	Brude Uruip
Brude Grid	Brude Urgrid
Brude Mund	Brude Urmund

In the History of the Picts, Scots and Britons, I pointed out that, in legend, Brutus was the legendary ancestor of the Britons, and that Brude is a variant of this name. I also pointed out that according to Julius Caesar the Celts chief god was the "All Father", and according to Ammianus Marcellinus the Celts believed that Hercules, son of Amphitryon, had many wives and was the father of many sons who gave their name to their territories. Linking these 3 legends Brude, a form of Brutus, is the British Hercules – the father god - and with the knowledge that the Celts believed in Land Gods and An or Anna was often quoted as another ancestress. The Ant part of the first name links to this eponymous Ann.

The translation then becomes

The Father of the sons of An	**The Father of our sons of An**
The Father of Lug	The Father of our Lug
The Father of Cant	The Father of our Cant
The Father of Gnith	The Father of our Gnith
The Father of Fecir	The Father of our Fecir
The Father of Cal	The Father of our Cal
The Father of Cint	The Father of our Cint
The Father of Fec	The Father of our Fec
The Father of Ru	The Father of our Ru
The Father of Gart	The Father of our Gart
The Father of Cinid	The Father of our Cinid
The Father of Uip	The Father of our Uip
The Father of Grid	The Father of our Grid
The Father of Mund	The Father of our Mund

The list also provides evidence of Ammianus' other statement about "Hercules" having sons by many wives, In the Norse language, the word for a Bride is Brud, in Gaelic this is Bride – both variants of the same word, so the word Brude serves many purposes, it tells us An is the Bride, "She" has a husband (B*rud de – of the Bride*), and "her" husband is the Father - Brude - of "her" son.

In the sequence of Brudes' An is the land from which life springs – In the 6th century, Gildas, in his discourse on the "Ruin and Conquest of Britain", tells us that inhabitants of Britain worshipped the land and features in the land. Perhaps it even exists in the name of the Decangli that Ptolomey names as occupying the south-west of England, or even in the name of "Germanic" tribe known as Angli.

The tribal names

In this list we can see several other tribal names that Ptolomey identified, along with the name of their "ancestral" god

1. An is the land itself – or at least that part of Britain occupied by the Pictish tribes. The name forms part of the ancient name that the Gaelic tribes called Scotland, i.e. Alban i.e. Alb An (perhaps Alb = North or High, An = Land).
2. Leo would be more familiar to us as Lug Lamfada (equivalent to the Welsh god Llew), quite obviously the founder of the tribe of Lugi.
3. Gant would be the ancestor of the Canti tribe.
4. Gnith would perhaps be the god of the Novantae (the inhabitants of Nithsdale)
5. Fecir would have to be the ancestor of the Venicones
6. Cal would be immediately identifiable as the ancestor of the Caledones
7. Cint would be the "father" of the Cintiaci
8. Fec would be the god of the Vacomagi
9. Ru is more familiar to us as Rueda, the founder of the Scottish nation. Here we have evidence of a link between the Scots and the Picts – More than likely is that this is evidence of a close relationship between Pictish & Scottish tribes. Is this the origin of the Irish legend that the Picts originally had Irish wives.

10. Gart could be the ancestor of the Carnonacae.
11. Cinid could possibly be the god of the Crenones (perhaps they have been misnamed and should be identified as Cinidones) or they may be another tribe entirely.
12. Uip is of course the ancestor of the Epidi.
13. Grid is the god of the Credones.
14. Mund we can identify as the ancestor of both the Dumnoni of Strathclyde and from this name establish a clear link to the inhabitants of Munster in Ireland. (This makes the Ivereni tribe of Munster a Fir Domnaan people).

Co-incidentally, for students of Geoffrey of Monmouth, the 12th century writer of "The History of the Kings of Britain", if you don't translate the name Brude, and read it in another form then you read Brud de ap Ant, or in Classical terms **Brut**us **of** son of **An**eas. All Geoffrey has done for his eponymous hero is add a classical ending onto the word Brud, allowing him to link his famous ancestor, and namer of Britain, Brutus to Ascanius, the son of the mythical exiled Trojan warrior and founder of Rome, Aeneas.

One of the interesting points in this list is that several northern tribes are missing from it – The Caerini, The Votadini, The Cornavi, The Smertae, The Taezali (also written as the Taexali) and The Selgovae. This is a significant omission as many of these tribes contribute extensively to the most unique symbol of Pictish art – the carvings on the Pictish stones.

This list then gives us our 26th & 27th major problems;

1) All of the tribes that are missing from the series of Brudes here, are the tribes that are most commonly associated with the Picts, in other words the Pictish

list does not include all of the Pictish tribes.

2) The Pictish list includes Northern British tribes but it also includes tribes from Southern Britain, such as the Crenones, as well as Scots (whose ancestor, according to Bede, was Rueda). So the Pictish tribal list also includes tribes that we do not associate with the Picts.

The Pictish king list does prove however, that they were made up of several tribes. It is probable that their numbers grew and fell as tribes joined and left them at various stages. In the 4th century Ammianus Marcellinus says that the Picts had combined to become only 2 tribes, the DiCalydones and Verturiones, often referred to as "super tribes" by modern historians. This is not apparent yet as this document lists 14 tribes individually.

This list, however, supports the notion that Pictish numbers were variable and that they were not a single race but made up of many different tribal groups at various times in their history.

Chapter 4: The Pictish Religion

In the 4th century we start to find physical evidence of Pictish beliefs in their monuments. These monuments appear during the 4th to the 9th century.

Distribution of Pictish Stones

Pictish stones appear in many areas of Scotland but in a very specific pattern as can be seen below.

This distribution pattern presents us with a problem in generalising these monuments as "Pictish".

The concentration lies in the North East. It mirrors the coast line of the North East above the Forth Clyde line, mainly round Fife, Angus as shown in the diagram below highlighting the path of the stones from the south east, northwards.

As can be seen very few of the stones lie outside this line and the stones, even the few that are on the West, appear close to, or within a few miles of the coast. In terms of land mass, the regions that the Stones appear in amounts to approximately 10% (or less) of the total land mass of Scotland.

The problem with this distribution pattern is that the Picts, the largest group of people, are almost evenly distributed throughout Scotland. There are Picts in the South East. South West, North East, North West and Central regions of Scotland, yet there are almost none of these monuments being produced in the South West and South East of Scotland – there are none in the Central region, and very, very few in the North West, and those in the Far North East are following the shape of the coastline.

The distribution indicates that there is a specific difference in the practices of the Picts in the areas where these stones exist, compared to the practices of the people where the stones don't appear. Yet they appear to be produced by some tribes that are both included and left out of the Pictish king list – such as the Lugi, Vacomagi, the Venicones, Cornavi, Smertae etc.

The reason for the construction of these stone monuments is unclear – cup and ring markings were engraved into stones by people across Britain in the prehistoric period but the practice had long since ceased by the 4th Century AD. The monuments left by the Picts are more advanced with some unusual characteristics, containing strange symbols. They also start to appear at a specific, relatively speaking, point in time, in the 4th century AD. This could indicate a major development in these areas at this time, e.g. a change of religion, a change in social structure, a change in the leadership, perhaps even a new settlement from Europe - the mysterious Attacoti mentioned by Ammianus Marcellinus perhaps (although I have stated in "The History of the Scots, Picts and Britons" that the Attacoti were likely to be the Romano-Britons rebelling against Rome).

When the carved stones were first discovered they were originally thought to be evidence of a "Viking" influence but the movement of the Scandinavian raiders of the 9th and 10th Centuries, would seem to rule this out. The Scandinavians attacked and gained footholds in the North, East, South and West of England, Wales, the Orkneys, Shetland, the Inner and Outer Hebrides, the West Coast of Scotland and Ireland. The North East Coast appears to be relatively unscathed. Could this be due to the "Belgic" settlement of the British coast Julius Caesar mentioned.

The lack of a later Scandinavian settlement would negate the notion of a 9th/10th century influence in the creation of Pictish Stone Monuments, yet there are parallels in Scandinavia with the beginning and end of their construction. In the 3rd century AD, the Scandinavians began constructing Runic stone monuments, with images drawn from their beliefs in Odin, Frigga, Thor etc. The following century the Picts seem to mimic this behaviour and create their own stone monuments. In the 8th century AD, the Runic monuments cease, the following century the Picts again mimic this and cease building stone monuments.

There is something unusual in the route used by 9th and 10th century "Viking" settlers in Scotland. This is the same route the 8th century historian Bede provided for the Picts.

They settle in the North East of England, they attack Lindisfarne monasteries, they conquer Northumbria, They take the Shetlands and the Orkneys, The Inner and Outer Hebrides, They take control of Kintyre, and some parts of the South West of Scotland, They take the Isle of Man, Dublin and other parts of Ireland, but during all of these "invasions", the East Coast of Scotland remains relatively untouched with only Caithness and Sutherland falling to them in the very far North. They appear to avoid the North East Coast of Scotland completely and instead sail their way to the west coast via one of the most treacherous routes imaginable around the far North of Scotland and the Orkneys – why?

The area that they avoid, or at least appear to avoid is the area in which we see the greatest concentration of Pictish stone monuments. Is the reason for this concentration due to the lack of "Viking" activity or is the lack of "Viking" activity due to the concentration of Pictish stones. If it is the latter then is there a relationship between the Scandinavians and the people in these areas. This would be the evidence so far

1. The Stones appear at or near coastal areas, where we expect there to be extensive sea travel and trade taking place. The Scandinavians were noted sea travellers, raiding and also trading extensively across Europe and the world.
2. The presence of Pictish stones indicates a difference in practices between the Picts that created them and the Picts that didn't create them.
3. The timeline for the construction of the runic stones in Scandinavia and the Pictish stones in Scotland parallel each other.
4. The Scandinavian raiders that reached Britain appear to avoid the areas where the stones appear in great numbers

Perhaps the most meaningful reason that a culture would not attack another culture is because they both believed that they shared the same beliefs. The differences in physical environment would create natural differences in clothing, design of implements, weapons, food etc. but the religion would remain very similar.

In the 3rd and 4th centuries AD, the most widespread religion in Northern Europe, was not Christianity, The chief areas of Northern Europe are the Scandinavian and Germanic regions where the belief in the Nordic/Germanic Gods – Odin/Woden, Freya, Frigga etc. was prevalent. Britain lies in the North of Europe, and the North East of Scotland lies directly opposite the Scandinavian regions.

We have 2 different contradictory Pictish traditions – one from the Romans that the Caledonians were red haired and long limbed, and may have crossed over from the Germanic regions. A much later one from Scandinavia that they were dark haired and small in stature. We have differences in Pictish practices between those of the South, West and East of Scotland. We have evidence of a "Celtic/Gaelic" influence in the Picts from the Irish legends - but Ireland lies on the west coast and any influence would primarily have been on Pictish tribes on the West Coast of Scotland (and probably the Central regions).

This supports the earlier notion that there are at least 2 (probably more) different and distinct Pictish groups, and not all of the "Pictish tribes" or the tribes that we think of as "Pictish" were included amongst them. The "Picts" on the North East Coast of Scotland were likely to retain the beliefs of their European neighbours directly opposite them – Northern Europeans – The Scandinavians. Is there anything in the Pictish stones that would support this?

Some of the earliest Pictish Stones exhibit a curious symbolism with 2 circular discs facing each other linked by

2 lines and a z symbol separating them, as in the following image from a stone at Aberlemno, in Angus.

Drawn out into basic form this would look something like the following image;

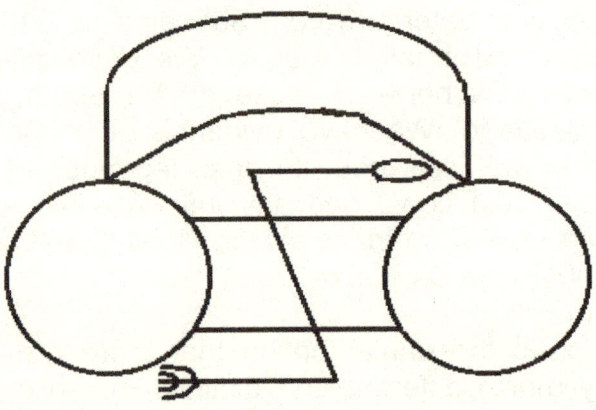

This is a very basic diagram – missing any accompanying details, but it does appear to be very similar to an engineering or architectural drawing.

It is as though an Elevation view (the side on view) of the crescent has been joined directly onto a Plan view (the top down view) of the two circles. The 2 parallel lines between the circles would represent the position of the Crescent between the 2 circles when looked at directly from above. The crescent is forming a bridge between the circles and linking them together. The Z symbol could be an arrow or rather a crooked spear going across the bridge barring or allowing entry. Contrary to popular opinion, many early civilisations, especially those that were familiar with sea travel (such as the Greeks and Persians) were already aware of the curvature of the Earth and that this was a "round" planet. The 2 circles could then be either 2 islands or 2 different worlds.

If the North East Picts shared a culture with the Scandinavians this symbol could represent the religion of Northern Europe, when the stone was carved. The 2 circles could be the worlds of Asgard and Midgard. The Z symbol is the spear Gungir. The crescent and parallel lines represent the Bifrost – the rainbow path that links both worlds. The snake that sometimes appears may be Jormungandr – the Midgard Serpent.

Other Pictish symbols that often appear in "Pictish" art also fall into line with the Norse Religion.

The Boar – The dead warriors of Valhalla feast on Boars every day in the great hall.
The fish – The Loki turns himself into a Salmon.
The wolf – The God Loki turns himself into a she-wolf. His son Fenrir is a monstrous wolf that has to be chained up by the gods
The horse – Asgard was constructed by a stallion, Svadilfari.
The goose – The goddess Frigga's symbol is the goose

And so on..

Another set of figures that often appear are the comb and mirror symbol (as can been seen on monuments such as the Dunnichen Stone, the Aberlemno stone etc.). If viewed as a mirror and comb they would seem to be out of place on a religious monument. But if they are viewed instead as a representation of other groups, like the 2 circles, then they could represent the other worlds of the Norse Religion. The mirror symbol would not be a mirror at all but 2 worlds - There are 5 lines on the comb symbol and these could indicate pathways to the other 5 worlds. This would be the 9 worlds of the Norse religion accounted for.

We know from Marcellinus that the Picts were split into 2 different groups and the distribution of the Pictish stones appears to support this view. St Patrick tells us that some of the Picts have reverted to an apostate state, and directly opposite the North East of Scotland lies the largest religious belief in Europe. In the 8th century Bede tells us that the Picts came from Scythia – meaning Scandinavia. It is possible that some of the Picts of North East Scotland either practised, or had adopted the religious practices of the Scandinavians directly opposite them.

Scandinavian or Celt?

The word Celt is derived from ancient Greek, and used to describe the people of Europe as "Keltoi". The term was not used in a racial sense, as modern DNA evidence has proved beyond doubt that most Celtic tribes were not genetically related, but to group multiple unrelated European tribes together under one banner.

The Greek Philosopher Timaeus (345-250BC) answers the question of whether the Picts were Celts or Scandinavians, when he refers to "Celts of the North Sea". Whether the people around the North East coast of Scotland were of

Scandinavian origin or not, they and the people living in the Scandinavian regions were both geographically on the North Sea and therefore, as Timaeus described "Celts", regardless of appearance, language or religion.

A Shared Scandinavian/Celtic Belief

There are remarkable similarities between the Celtic Gods and the Norse Gods, (some of which are named in an online article by Thor Ewing
(http://www.historicalarts. co.uk/articles/sinsear/the_birth_of_lugh.html))

- The name of the chief Scandinavian god Odin and its Anglo-Saxon variant Wōden is thought to derive from a reconstructed Proto-Germanic noun *wōđanaz, itself deriving out of the adjective *wōđaz, which is related to the Old Irish word fáith. This indicates an ancient connection between the Norse Gods and the Gaelic language.

- In Norse mythology Odin is also known as the All Father, In Julius Caesar's biography he spoke of the the Gauls claim to be descended from the "Dis Pater" - the All Father. In Irish mythology the Dagda, is also known as Eochaid Ollathair – the all Father.

- The Dagda and Odin are both also said to wear cloaks

- Lugh Lamfada (and the Gallic equivalent Lugus), is associated with a spear, and ravens, as is Odin

- Odin has one eye, while the grandfather god of Lugh, Balar is also one eyed. At the battle of Magh Tuiredh, Lugh Lamfada chants with one eye closed.

- There is a similarity in the name of Lugh's grandfather Balar, to the name of Odin's father Borr and grandfather Buri. There is even greater similarity in the name of Odin's son Baldur.

- Lugh Lamfada was the leader of the gods, as is Odin

- Lugh Lamfada and Odin are both associated with the Roman God Mercury.

- The names of Lugh and the Norse God Loki, foster son of Odin, are similar and neither father is named

There are many more similarities, but in essence the Celtic Gods appear to have the same roots as the Norse Gods. Their stories, and possibly names, diverged at some point due to many factors e.g. passage of time, integration with other beliefs (civilisations such as Rome, Greece, Persia etc. merged beliefs with other people - Chronos, became Saturnus, Heracles, became Hercules etc., while their own beliefs were also maintained – Romulus and Remus etc.). Medieval Christian monks, wrote down. but also changed, and added new, stories to the pantheon of these early Gods, making the deities more human and vulnerable, and therefore less powerful and godlike.

A shared religious culture lends credence to Bede's assertion that some Picts – those that he would have been in contact with from Jarrow (in the North East of England) - originated from "Scythia". The stones may have provided physical evidence of a "shared culture" whether it was just a religious belief or a genuine genetic relationship, which may have played a part in preventing the North East from being settled by "Vikings".

Chapter 5: A Combined Symbol

There may even be more to the stones than just a religious symbolism. Many of the stones have additional details on them, which may link to the structure and leadership of the Picts. We may be able to see this in the carving on the the Dunnichen Stone, a Class I Pictish monument dating between the 6th and 8th century. I have highlighted these details

On the inside of one circle we have 7 wave patterns, and what appears to be 6 or possibly 7 wave patterns inside the other. Ammianus Marcellinus tells us the Picts were split into 2 tribes in the 4th century – the Dicalydones and the Verturiones, but he treats the Scots as a separate group. The Scots appear in the Pictish King list under the Brude entry for Ru(eda). If we then ignore the Scots, the 2 circles could represent these 2 groups of Picts - We have 6 Northern tribes missing from the Pictish King List and at least 6 crests inside one circle. The missing tribes are the Taezali, the Cornavi, the Caerini, the Smertae, the Selgovae and the Votadini. These 6 tribes would be the Verturiones. The 7 tribes of the Pictish King list would belong to the

Dicalydones. These would be the Canti (DeCantae), the Caledones, the Venicones, the Cintiaci, the Vacomagi, the Lugi and the Novantae. Both Pictish groups are then made up of unrelated tribes, with very different backgrounds.

A strange looking solitary figure is carved above the circles. Looking at this from a distance - and these stones were probably intended to be viewed at a distance - it could looks like a hat or a helmet, perhaps with some form of crest, horsehair/feather etc. attached to the crown. This would represent that both groups were united under one figure. The "King" of the Picts. The Dunnichen stone however has been exposed over the centuries and suffers from substantial wear. It may also be a mountain, with a cloud hiding the peak, but there is something else that does spring to mind that would connect it to a real Pictish monarch.

Dunnichen is traditionally the place where the battle of Dun Nechtan, or Nechtansmere, is thought to have occurred. At the battle of Dun Nechtan c. 685AD the Pictish king Breide Mac Bili is described as fighting for his "*grandfather's kingdom*", and defeated his cousin, the Northumbrian king Ecgfrith, thereby releasing the Picts from their overlordship by Northumbria. Is there something in the figure that could link it to this event. Apart from a hat/helmet with a crest, or a mountain with a cloud, another natural feature that rises into the air, would be a tree, If the figure is a tree, the lines could represent the bark, and the mysterious object at the top, the foliage.

The Gaelic word for a sacred tree is Bile, instead of Breide Mac Bili, we could create a play on words and write Breide Mac Bile. This name would link Breide back to the figure at the top of the stone, and the stone could represent Breide's victory and be announcing that Breide Mac Bile is the king of all the Picts. We can see similar patterns in other "Pictish" artefacts that have been uncovered, such as the one below on a plaque found amongst the 7th century Norrie's Law Pictish hoard

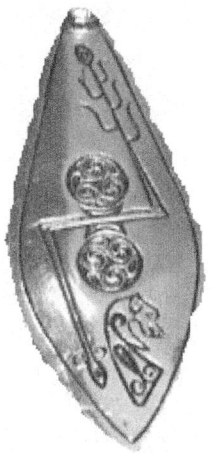

On this artefact we see similar figures to those that appear on the Dunnichen Stone, although the double disc symbol does seem slightly different with swirls rather than waves.

The image I am interested in is the one that represents the head – the hat/helmet. It is clearly different from the Dunnichen stone and shows the head of a Dog or a Hound One sixth century king stands out whose name has a definite link to this figure - Breide Mac Maelcon.

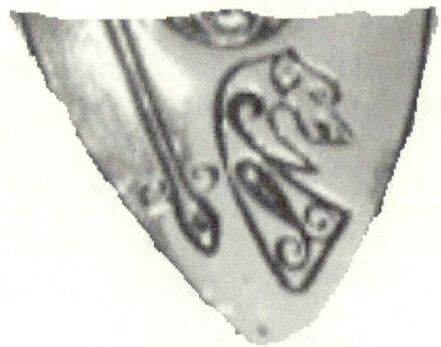

Breide is a variant of Brude, meaning Father of, Mac is Gaelic meaning son of and Maelcon is the name. Breide Mac Maelcon means the father of the son of Maelcon. Breide Mac Maelcon appears to be a play on words. The name Maelcon is a derivation of the Gaelic Maol, meaning servant or follower of (or even bald) and Cun, the hound.

The plaque found in the Norrie's Law Hoard must tie itself to Breide Mac Maelcon somehow – maybe these were the people of the "hound", or led by the "hound". The symbolism links the Pictish people, their "pagan" beliefs, and their kings together. The "hat" appears to be related to the use of the name Breide, or Brude, on both the Dunnichen stone and the Norries Law horde. It is a shape we have seen before in chapter 2, the triangular shape of Britain that had the top 1/3 rotated 90 degrees - this shape represents the the land of Britain and links to the "ancestor" god of the "Britons" - Brude. The "hat" represents the Pictish kings that bear the title, "Breide"– the "British" father. The symbols on the stone are then composite, serving many purposes rather than just one.

Composite symbols evolve and change over time and so we continue to get further variations in the Pictish stone carvings. We can see yet another variation appearing in the following image of another Pictish stone at Aberlemno.

In this stone we have a snake symbol instead of a hat/helmet, but like the Norries Law hoard plaque and the Dunnichen Stone, the symbol appears at the "spear tip" end of the Z form. The snake image could link the stone back to another monarch on the Pictish King List, Nechtan nepos Ui Erb. Erb is a variant of the Gaelic word earc which itself is an alternative spelling of the word Erc the ancestor of the "sons of Erc" that took Scotland. Earc is also the Gaelic name for an unspecified speckled or striped animal such as a reptile , lizard or snake. So here we have another link between the images carved into the Pictish Symbol Stones, the Pictish King List, and yet again a familial link in the name as Ui, is the Gaelic word for Grandson.

Clearly the Symbol Stones are talking of the monarchs, or, at least, the families, that rule over the Picts, the symbol immediately next to the "spear tip" of the Z form must represent the "monarch". We can see examples of other Pictish leaders on other stones, such as the horse figure on the fragment of a Class I Pictish stone at Inverurie in Angus. This symbol links to the name of a number of early kings –

Eochaid and variants such as Eachdach etc., while the Norwegian word for horse, hest, is contained in the name of other early Pictish kings such as Drest (i.e Dr**hest)**, There is further evidence of this in the Ogham inscriptions that start to appear on stones around the 6th - 8th century AD. Various references to kings such as Nechtan, and sons of Talorc & Drostan appear at Aboyne, Altyre, Bressey, Latheron and Lunnasting.
(*http://web.onetel.net.uk/~hibou/Pictish Inscriptions.html*)

The symbols and the inscriptions appear to link to names in the Pictish King List. These names are likely to be "Over-Kings" of the Pictish territories, rather than local leaders. The Pictish Symbol stones appear to be a method of communicating the name of the "overking" to the locals.

The images demonstrate in physical form, a link between the territories, the "ancestor god", the incumbent king - a representation of this god – the "father of all of the tribes of An", and their religion. The double disc represents the 2 Pictish groups, and inside the discs are swirls or waves that represent the individual tribes of the Picts. The comb & mirror symbol possibly represents the remaining peoples of North Britain, including the Scots, so underneath the king there are 19 different tribes – so we have evidence of a "Northern coalition" of tribes and that Pictish and Scottish tribes are under the rule of one "overking" - at least in theory, if not practice.

The symbol stones appear to be of a composite design merging religious beliefs, ancestor gods and the individual tribes together, so they form a triple function. There are many examples of composite symbols like this from ancient to modern times, the merging of the crowns of Upper & Lower Egypt, The British and American Flags etc., and they vary in design as they are subject to changes in territory, populations etc. This mixing of familiar religious symbolism with a leadership structure is not unique. In medieval societies, it was believed that Kings were appointed by God, they were anointed with religious oils at coronations, with declarations made in front of God by senior figures of their churches – Arch Bishops, Bishops etc., using holy relics. Their ancestry was traced back to Jesus, Noah and ultimately God himself – all of which was designed to enforce and reinforce the divine right of kings to rule. It would be a sin and would ultimately be a crime against God, carrying horrendous penalties in this world and the next, to injure, kill, replace or overthrow them. Using religion to reinforce a right to rule to prevent an overthrow was a well used mechanism in the ancient world, and is still being used in some societies today. The Picts were simply using the same mechanism.

It's almost propaganda, and the reason that these stones appear in these areas is that these were the ones furthest away, that were most in need of reminding who was in charge, most likely to "rebel". it's a way of dominating the landscape and communicating with the locals, and the reason they need communicating with by symbolism, maybe they didn't speak the same language in these areas – they spoke the "Pictish" language. Like the famous Rosetta stone that was used to decipher Egyptian hieroglyphics, the stone was created to pass on the same information to different groups of people in the same area. The Rosetta stone had hieroglyphic script for the Egyptian population, Greek for the Greek population (or rather the Macedonian descendants of Alexander's army) and Latin for the occupying Roman Army population – all of them resident in Egypt at the same time. 2 methods of communication on a single stone means that amongst the Picts of the 6th century were "Irish" and non-"Irish" populations. The Picts were not a heterogeneous population by the 6th century.

This probably means that there was a language spoken near the coastal areas of the North East, that was limited to some groups of people, rather than all of the Picts. It could be a variant of the Scandinavian language, it could be a dialect problem, or it could have been an unfamiliar variant of a P/Q Celtic language – the Cornavi are a coastal tribe found in both the North and the South of Britain and nowadays the language of the Southern Cornavi - "Cornish" - is recognised as a language in it's own right rather than just a variant of Welsh – yet it is not mentioned by Bede or even Henry of Huntingdon. From Bede we see some elements of P Celtic words in the language of the Picts – he describes how Penfahel was the Pictish word for the "town" the "English" called Penneltun – The welsh word Pen or Peann meaning Head or chief. In the North East we see the Welsh/Brythonic word Aber, meaning at the mouth or head of a river, equivalent to to the Gaelic word Inver, in placenames such as Aberdeen, Aberfeldy etc. It's possible a form of "Cornish" was spoken by the Northern Cornavi, and may have had Scandinavian elements. A Scandinavian link may be the contributory factor in the lack of Viking settlement. Scandinavian though, was not the language of the leadership, who were the P and Q Celtic peoples of the series of Brudes in the Pictish King List.

We could have up to 3 classes of Picts – Britons, Gaels and some "Scandinavian" elements. These groups would have become mixed over time leading to the possibility of at least 27 different subgroups of Gael-Briton, Scandinavian–Gaels, Briton-Scandinavian etc. With various groups dominating over other groups in their region, this could explain the Picts being split between 7 different kingdoms (mormaerdoms) in later years. This mix would lead to difficulties of communication, not just because of language barriers but also dialect and religious divisions. This would then explain why there was a need to construct these monuments

The stones start to appear around the mid - late 4th century, which coincides with the "Barbarian conspiracy" mentioned by Marcellinus, and the campaigns against the "Barbarians" by the Roman Commanders, Theodosius in 369AD and Stilicho c.390AD. Roman writers have it that the Picts suffered a great slaughter. Common sense dictates that as their leaders took part in battle, they were likely to have been amongst the dead, creating a power vacuum. The stones construction starting at this time is not a coincidence. They are symbolic of a change in the hierarchy, one requiring communication by a physical image linking their beliefs, social structure, to the new regime, rather than words, because of a communication difficulty – after all "a picture paints a thousand words". The new regime would need to be drawn from those that did not suffer the wrath of Rome, maybe even a "puppet" ruler that the Roman army could use to pacify the Northern territories. A "King" probably drawn from their Gaelic relatives, those that were "curbed" by the Roman Army, rather than left "dying" - the Scots. It is around this time that the Senchus fer'n Alban begins it's tale, with the Mac Erc's arriving from "Ireland" and, as it states, taking over Alba. Whether the MacErc's were real or not, it was a method to explain how the Scots gained control of all of the North.

This means there is no such thing as a people or race of "Picts", it wasn't a singular group. It related to many different people, with different beliefs and different languages – a multi ethnic Britain was identified in the 1st century by Tacitus when he stated that;

"The reddish hair and large limbs of the Caledonians proclaim a German origin; the swarthy faces of the Silures, the tendency of their hair to curl, and the fact that Spain lies opposite, all lead one to believe that Spaniards crossed in ancient times and occupied that part of the country. The

peoples nearest to the Gauls likewise resemble them".

With Scandinavia on the East Coast, Ireland on the West Coast, The Orkney and Shetlands in the North, (Russia further North) and a mix of unrelated British tribes in the South. The conclusion is that the Picts of Scotland were a mix of different groups, that allied against the Roman Invasion, between the 1st and late 3rd Century AD.

Chapter 6 : Indigenous or Not?

The belief in the Picts being an indigenous population is primarily a modern invention. The earliest sources from Gildas, Bede, Nennius are all in agreement that they were from a "foreign" culture. There may be some support for the view that, although the leadership was Celtic, the general population over which they ruled could be indigenous. There are several reasons why this is unlikely.

The Population Argument

Britain, does not, and has never had an indigenous population. The first settlers were nomadic groups of hunter gatherers that stayed for short periods of time and left. The first set of permanent settlers arrived around 5000-4000BC. But these would have been small individual neolithic communities arriving over the next thousand or so years, rather than an organised mass migration. Next would have been Mesolithic settlers, and so on, until around 400BC the La Tene Era Celts arrived. Is it possible that these early Neolithic groups could have come from islands off the northern coast of Scotland, and through simply increasing their numbers over the next few thousand years, evolved into the Northern Pictish tribes. It is an idea that many historians support but it has major flaws.

The Numerical Argument

Around 400AD, at the end of the Roman rule in Britain the population of Scotland was around 172414, (This figure was worked out in my previous book, the History of the Scots, Picts and Britons and took into account the population fluctuations – growth and decline in the UK until 1881AD). If we accept the view of History presented by William Skene et al, and the Picts had settled in Northern

Britain, the Scots did not arrive until 500AD, and the "Britons" of Strathclyde, were really "proto-Picts", the Picts would have accounted for around 17 out of the 18 mainland "Scottish" tribes named by Ptolomey – around 94.4% of the population, but this percentage works against the arguments for them to be descended from the earliest settlers of Britain, or coming from the Orkneys. Settlement of Britain began between 5000-4000 BC. If growth occurred linearly by a factor of 2 per generation, then it would just require between 635 and 650 people to arrive by 4000BC.

It doesn't appear to be a large number of people today, but for 4000BC, and an estimated world population of 28 million, that is an enormous no. Although unlikely, the number is not so outrageous as to be impossible, particularly if we accept that these people were migrating in smaller numbers over long periods of time. That would be the "historians" general argument for the notion of an indigenous Pictish people.

The problem with this idea is that growth does not occur linearly but exponentially. This can be proved statistically from modern studies of increasing/declining populations using sources such as census statistics. The reason for exponential growth is due to a large number of factors including, but not limited, to the following;

1. Environmental conditions - periods of drought, famine
2. The population will include a percentage of older people, that will not produce any further children.
3. A percentage of individuals with fertility problems
4. A percentage of people suffering from life limiting diseases,
5. Lack of effective medical care in many regions
6. High Infant Mortality rates in children.

7. Shorter life spans
8. Warfare
9. Deliberate and accidental killings

For the prehistoric period there have been a number of studies carried out on the population growth from 10,000AD until the present time.

(For those of you interested in taking a look at these figures and the various studies that produced them, more information can be found on Wikipedia at the following URL address - https://en.wikipedia.org/wiki/World_population_estimates#Deep_prehistory).

These studies are in general agreement with exponential growth in the prehistoric period. It takes well over a thousand years for the population to increase by double, as can be seen in the following table where I calculated the rate of growth, using the estimates for world population, produced by the History Database of the Global Environment (HYDE).

World Population	Hyde	Rate of Growth
5000BC	18	Not Applicable
4000BC	28	1.56
3000BC	45	1.61
2000BC	72	1.60
1000BC	115	1.60
0BC	188	1.63
1000AD	295	1.57
		Average 1.59

Thus we have a rate of change every thousand years of 1.59, or by rounding up this figure (for an easier calculation) 1.6. So starting around 500AD where the population would have increased in the 100 years from 400AD by 0.16% (i.e. A tenth of the 1.6 rate every thousand years). The starting population would be around 200,000. Knowing that the present day population of Orkney is 0.39% of the total population of Scotland, we can then use this figure to plot the no. of people required to produce an indigenous population of Picts arriving from Orkney in the earliest prehistoric periods, in both tabular and graphical form;

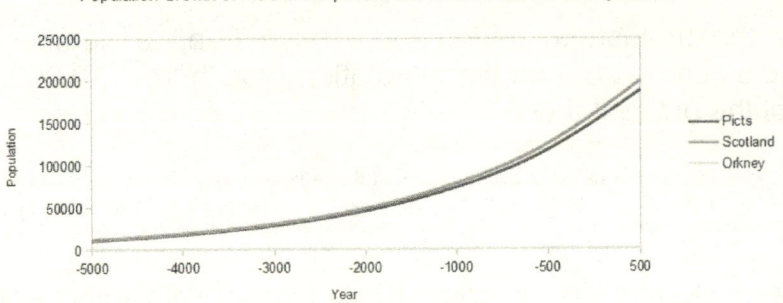

Around 18013 people would have to have arrived on Mainland Scotland in 4000BC, more than 240 times the population of the Orkneys. At that time, this would have been the equivalent of just over 6% of Europe's entire population (approx just over 2.7million) – almost 100 times higher than in the present day, as Scotland only accounts for 0.07% of Europe's population.

It may also be a very conservative estimate of the discrepancy as HYDE provides some of the highest estimates, a number of other studies have suggested that there was a lower world population of only 7 million.
(http://www.worldhistorysite.com/population.html),

A lower figure of 7 million would mean up to almost 24% of Europe's population would have to be resident in Scotland. The Orkney's simply never got anywhere near producing the number of people required to populate Scotland with Picts, and neither could Scandinavia – The combined population of Norway, Sweden, Denmark, Iceland, Greenland and the Faroe Islands only amounts to 3% of Europe's population, this is exactly half of the number that would need to have migrated from there to populate Scotland with Picts. It just wouldn't be realistic for the Picts to have come from one particular region of Europe.

There are a couple of counter arguments of course.

1. Not all of Scotland's "tribes" were Picts so it does not require the numbers or percentages specified.

    This would be the "traditionalists" argument. We have included too many tribes as Picts – there are 3 groups in Scotland in 500AD – Scots, Britons and Picts. Unfortunately it still doesn't work as this would mean at the very least 1/3 of the population would still be Picts, so 80 times the population of Orkney has to arrive and a mass migration from Scandinavia of around 2/3 of it's population has to happen – something for which there is no evidence.

    But the traditionalist view also means that only a small number of the population are Scots, even in Argyll, with the Britons being limited to Strathclyde. This leaves between 3/4 and 2/3 of the population of Scotland as Picts. So we are pretty much back where we started, needing around 180 times the population of Orkney, more than 4% of the population of Europe and still way more than the entire population of Scandinavia.

2. It does not take into account the migration from European countries to the new world.

    This was taken into consideration in the figures but even if it wasn't it would work against the indigenous theory. For example around 73% of the U.S population (565 million) has European Ancestry, however the majority of these, approx 56% of North America's population, has a UK origin. with Germany

being the next largest. The Scandinavian countries account for a very few of "new world" settlers.
(https://en.wikipedia.org/wiki/European_Americans)

The effects this would have had on the prehistoric population in Scandinavia would be very, very small, negligible. Essentially their population would be more or less as it was. It was the UK that experienced the largest migration of any other European country with people leaving for many colonies all over the world, including the U.S, Canada, New Zealand, Australia, Africa, India etc. – If any population was going to be larger it would have been the population in the UK and Scotland, so it would require even greater numbers to migrate from Europe to Britain in the prehistoric period to populate Scotland with "Picts"

The statistical argument completely rules out any notion of the Picts as a single indigenous population – The population of Scotland before during and after the Roman Occupation was a multi-racial mix of many or all of the multiple groups of settlers from multiple periods of British pre-history. The Picts, or at least the populations under their control, were mongrels – just as we all are today.

The Genetic Argument

In the Roman Period, there was no origin provided for the Picts, other than the one suggested by Tacitus for the Caledonians - that their appearance indicated that they probably arrived from north of the Rhine, possibly Germania. Their contemporaries report that they were later arrivals to Britain, and that would link them to the groups of settlers from North of the Rhine and other remote islands, that also settled in Gaul around the same time – La Tene Era Celts.

Pictish Red Hair

We can't really argue with Tacitus, he is the only documented eye witness to their appearance. He says that the Caledonians were red haired and later Roman writers identified the tribe as Picts. Is it possible that their appearance was due to a unique Pictish gene?. The red haired population of Scotland is around 13%, the highest anywhere in the British Isles, including Ireland.

The Caledonians were roughly 1 of 18 tribes in Scotland – i.e. 5.5% of the Population, less than half of 13%. The Caledonians therefore, although significant, could not account for the 13% of the Red-Haired Population of Scotland on their own. The Red Hair gene had to be carried by other tribes. And there is testimonial evidence from Roman sources supporting this.

The warrior Queen Boudica of the Southern British tribe of the Iceni, was said to be red haired. But this would make red hair a "British" rather than a "Pictish" trait. Although red hair accounts for less of a percentage (approximately 10%) of the population of England, It means, numerically than the numbers of red haired people, in Wales, Scotland and Ireland combined are much, much less than in England. The chances are that if you see a red haired person they are statistically more likely to be English than any other nationality within the British Isles.

This means that if the Caledonians came as Picts carrying the red hair gene, then other tribes across the length and breadth of the British Isles came with them, from the same origin, and the largest number of them settled in England, which is not an area that is associated to the Picts. This means that the Caledonians gene pool was by no means unique, and does not qualify as a "Pictish" feature by itself.

In fact, it does the opposite, and seems to link them to the La Tene Era Celtic migration into Europe from the areas North of the Rhine.

The Dark Haired Pict

In the 12th century in the Historia Norwegia we get a completely different description of the Picts, to any one we have seen before. it is a description that contradicts everything we have been told about them from their Roman and British contemporaries.

The Historia describes how the Picts were small in stature and lived underground. It is from this history that we get the supporting notion of Picts being a prehistoric indigenous people, the builders of soutterains, yet it contradicts everything that we were told about them during the period that they were a "real" force majeure.

But it does have some value. The Picts were a coalition of different tribes, we can see this in the Pictish King list, of these only a small portion could have exhibited the features of the Caledonians. If we align this to the knowledge that we have a divided, not a united, Pictish society, different languages, accents, different religions, traditions, practices – we can see how this Scandinavian view of the Picts came about.

The Scandinavians looking across at the North East of Scotland, mainly settle on the west coast of Scotland, they avoided the North East – principally because they probably already had an established relationship with several groups around the coastal regions. To them those people they were looking at were the same as themselves, so the Picts had to be those people that they didn't look like – those groups or people that they were least like.

The stereotypical view of the Scandinavian is that they are tall, fair haired, lived above ground, and enjoy "open air" pursuits like hunting, sports and basically anything that involved some form of physical exertion. The Picts, often the enemy in the early sources, could not have looked like them, so they had to be people that exhibited the exact opposite characteristics.

It was this Scandinavian view of the Picts that put the thought of the Picts being a prehistoric indigenous people in the minds of Victorian and 20th century historians.

Paradoxically however, in the minds of medieval historians, like Geoffrey of Monmouth and the Irish and Scandinavian annalists it is an exactly opposite view. If you read their documents, you find that the people that are conquered by the likes of Brutus, the sons of Milid etc. Odin – are often considered to be Giants, much bigger than the people that have defeated them. To the medieval annalist people are getting smaller, not larger. It sort of ties in with the ideas that we find in Bede's work, and to some extent in Gildas, where the modern world is much worse than it was in the past, which is then being looked at with "rose-tinted spectacles".

The "Pictish" stones argument

One of the arguments that is used to support the Picts as an indigenous people is that of the appearance of Pictish stones. I have dealt with some of these in previous chapters but these stones cannot provide any such evidence

1. Neolithic Cup and Ring symbols carved into stonework are found all across Europe and Britain during the prehistoric period. There is no evidence supporting a continuous practice of rock art in those

areas dominated by "Pictish" tribes.

2. The carving of Pictish stones commences in the 4th century AD, thousands of years after the first settlers arrived in Britain, long after the Roman Invasion and many years after the first mention of Picts by Eumenius in 297AD.

3. Pictish stones are a later creation than the Runic stones that the non-indigenous populations of Scandinavia start to produce in the late 3rd century. There are some indications that the creation of Pictish stones may have been influenced or inspired by this earlier artwork.

4. The carving of Pictish stones is not being carried out by all of the Pictish tribes. Their distribution is concentrated mainly on the North East coast of Scotland, directly opposite North European regions such as Scandinavia. Their presence indicates a link to the people or religions of Northern Europe.

5. The figures and characters on later stones that appear to look like figures from early Phonecia, are initiated over a thousand years after Phonecia ceased to exist (around 800BC). If this artwork presented evidence of early prehistoric settlement from Phonecia, then why didn't these characters appear on carved stones before the 4th century AD?. It is plausible that that there had been some influence from classical sources, but this may not be unexpected. The stones appear near coastal regions, where we would expect to see some form of trade occurring with sailors and merchants from other countries. In addition many of these figures appear on stones that include Christian iconography.

Some of the early Christian missionaries came from other European regions, while many of the native British Christian missionaries and priests were educated in other countries such as Gaul, where we would expect to see Roman and classical style art. In short there are many other reasons for the influencing of "Pictish" art that do not require the artists to have an ancient origin.

Chapter 7: Problems and Contradictions

Wherever we go with the Picts we encounter problems with defining them.

1. Lack of detail

The Romans encounter them but the only information they give us is that they caused a lot of trouble, they are often grouped with the Scots, but while Romans kill Picts, they only curb Scots – so they are having to treat the Picts differently. We get the name of one Pictish tribe – the Caledoni, yet they tell us that there were other tribes, and that by the mid 4th century there were 2 different groups. They provide one description that we can use that the Caledoni are red haired and long limbed, and suggest a Germanic origin for them, which possibly links them to the later La Tene Celts that also settled in Gaul

What the Romans don't provide is the one thing that we think we know, the location of all of the Picts – we get the location of only one tribe, the Caledoni from Ptolomey, and the name of the battle fought against them in Britain by Agricola, at Mons Grapius. That's pretty much all we actually have on solid facts from Rome, most of what else we have is based on assumptions.

2. Contradictory Behaviour

The British sources give us a confusing tale. In the 5th century they tell us that some soldiers of supposed British kings, were in alliance with the Picts and the Scots and they all engaged in slave trading of Christian slaves. They tell us that some had gone from being pagan to Christian and back to pagan again. In the sixth century they tell us that the Picts were from "overseas" like the Scots, and attacked the Britons using coracles to travel across sea-rivers. In doing so they fail to mention any previous British-Pictish-Scots alliances. In the 7th century they tell us that in the sixth century the Pictish religious leaders were still Druids, in spite of many prior conversions by earlier missionaries such as Ninnian and Palladius.

They also tell us that the descendants of the Scottish king Aidan MacGabran had taken control of Fortrenn, the Pictish kingdom, yet other historians claim that the Scots had been besieged and conquered by the Picts, even though the Picts themselves were under the control of Northumbria until 685AD.

In the eighth century we get yet another story – this time we get their origins as Scythia and a mysterious practice of matrilineal succession, 400 years after they get mentioned by Eumenius, and over 700 years since the Roman Occupation began. Even more confusingly is that we are told they arrived in Ireland in only a few warships, making them entirely male and few in number. This tale is very similar to that of the MacErc's in Scotland, and the arrival in England of the first Germanic invaders – the Jutish princes Hengest and Horsa. A small band of entirely male warriors arriving on "foreign" soil in a few warships.

3. Internal Divisions

The Picts themselves – the distribution of their stones tells us that there are divisions amongst them, and they do not share the same customs. The instigation of symbol stones the 4th century AD tells us that this is something new – it may be part of some new belief system and a change in the hierarchy. This may be part of the reason for their division into 2 groups that Marcellinus attested to.

It also tells us that they may have communications with or a relationship with Scandinavia, perhaps even share a religious ideology. In the 9th century when the stones stop appearing, we are being informed that some important Pictish customs are no longer being practised, that their adherence to the unique practices had ceased and their society, or at least one significant part of it, had or was undergoing a dramatic change.

4. Mixed Genealogies

In the 10th century we may be getting something more from them through the Pictish king list, The series of Brudes tells us that they followed the traditional origin tales suggested by Geoffrey of Monmouth – that their ancestor was known as Brude (Brutus), that they believed they were descended from someone known as An – which strangely enough links them to the Northern European genealogies of the Saxon warlords of Southern England, who claimed descent from

"Beli the great, husband of Anna"

The list though names multiple tribes amongst the Picts, including the Scots, through the presence of Ru(eda), which seems to confirm that the Scots and Picts did have some form of alliance. Some of the tribes that appear in the list were based in Southern Britain, indicating that the Picts were spread throughout Britain and not limited to the Northern part – but it does not include many other Northern tribes, so it seems to be limited to only one group of "Picts" – again this may confirm a division between two groups, polarising into different societies.

5. Shared Monarchs

In the latter part of the Pictish king list we the see that the reigns of their kings directly correlate with the reigns of the Dal Riadic Scottish kings, and that they may share the same mythical ancestor – Erp/Erc – the "snake" - the symbol that appears at the top of the Aberlemno Stone.

Pictish King List	**Dalriadic Monarchs**
Drust (d 478)	Fergus (501? 3 year reign)
Talore (478-482)	Angus Mor?
Nechtan (482-506)	Domangart Ness' son (d 506)
Drest Gurthinmoch (506-36)	Comgall (506-537)
Drust son of Gyrom (536-558)	Gabran (d 559)
Brude Mac Maelcon (558-584)	Conall (559-)

In the Irish tales Erc was a woman, the mother of the High King Muiredach Mac Erc, whose reign corresponds to that of the Mac Erc's of Dal Riada, The eighth century Senchus Fer 'Alban tells us that there were seven brothers – one of them was called Muiredach. Erc being a woman contradicts the Senchus but it does match with the Irish tales and it does seem to correspond with Bede's statement that the Picts did have at least some kings descended from an Irish mother.

6. Sudden Disappearance

In medieval times we find out that the Picts disappeared from written history between 889 and 900AD. In line with the ceasing of the construction of Pictish stones. By 1140AD we find out that in a relatively short period of time, their society, practices, customs, religions and language had disappeared completely.

7. Composite Groups

This is what statistical analysis of Population growth tells us. It would be mathematically impossible for the Picts to be a single indigenous people, In order to grow to the size of population that they had in Northern Scotland, they would have to have included, merged with and married into, other native and non native tribes over many, many thousands of years. So they just cannot be a single "race". That would be statistically impossible.

8. Unrealistic Origin Myths

Having identified problems with the facts, we start to look at rather fanciful legends.

1. They took wives of the Irish and that was the reason for matrilineal succession. There has to be some truth in this – statistically they had to marry into, mate with, merge with other tribes in the British Isles. The Pictish king list does indicate that some early kings descended from a "mythical" female ancestor – Erc.

2. They came from Thracia – yet again there may be some truth to this. The Picts were not a single group of People, there were likely to be multiple origins for different tribe, originating from many migrations to Britain from the Neolithic period, up to and including the Celtic period.

3. They came from Scythia – again nothing untoward in that Belief – The Druids of Gaul confirmed in the 4th century AD that a number of tribes migrated from the North of the Rhine and outer islands of Europe. This is confirmed by archaeological evidence and uncovering of La Tene era artefacts around Europe.

4. The list of Kings descending from Parthalon – one of

the early kings whose people settled Ireland - This one I agree is fanciful. It is likely to be a mixed up tale with legends arising from many sources trying to combine into one shared culture. There is evidence of a relationship between Scots and Picts and this serves the purpose of merging the 2 groups eventually into one people under the control of Scots kings. The series of Brudes is basically a tribal list and not a list of kings, so the names that appear earlier than this are probably drawn from some of the individual tribal customs and beliefs and simply got added to each other,

There are many more legends relating to the Picts and this document could go on for hundreds, if not thousands of pages, but the purpose of this is to demonstrate that there is some truth in many of the legends but, as with all family histories, many of them are the result of misinterpretation and misrepresentation of the facts.

Chapter 8: What does the name Pict mean

This is one of the biggest bones of contention for the multitudes of academics that study the Picts. Was it a native name, was it given to them by the Romans, does it mean painted people, does it mean ancestor. In truth most of this doesn't really matter, it was a name that dark age people recognised, and probably feared, and that, ultimately, was all that was really important to them.

It was not until the third century AD that anyone talks of the Picts – after this the name becomes a commonplace term for the tribes that were causing most of the trouble for the Roman Armies, Generals and Emperors, and Romano-British. The term is always used in an almost derogatory way.

"and other Picts" (as though they were not important enough to name any other tribes by name)

"the dying face of the Pict" (to show how much the Romans could control them and how they treated them)

*foul hordes of Picts" (to show how nasty, violent and numerous they were)

"apostate Pict" (to show how irreligious they were – maybe how fickle and untrustworthy – first converting to Christianity and then back to paganism)

The Coalition of Pictish tribes

We know that Picts were not a single group. The assumption that the Pictish coalition lay just in the North does not correspond to the tribes named in the Pictish King List, so we are left with a problem. Every one talks about the Picts as though it was one group, so maybe we should look at the way the tribes coalesced.

Many British tribes had caused problems for the Roman Empire throughout their occupation of Britain, the trouble took place both inside and outside the Roman occupied territory, but the Picts seem to bear the brunt of the Roman venom. By the mid 4th century we appear to be getting to a point where individual tribes are not worth mentioning. After Marcellinus talks of the 2 groups of Picts as Dicalydones and Verturiones, even this separation seems to cease. All of the British tribes causing trouble for the Romans were classed as Picts.

The terminology of Pict

We should really consider the word Pict as a term, more than a word, at least in so far as the way it is getting used. Pict is a term that somehow separates these people from Romano-British civilisation and the key here is is the word civilisation, The Romans, like the Greeks before them believed they were a civilised people, they read books, studied science, medicine, taught their children etc., (forgetting, of course, the public murders and executions that they carried out in the name of entertainment in their arenas). The name Pict somehow denotes a group of people that do not conform to "civilised" society, and only one word really springs to mind – they were "barbarian"

But that would only provide a part of the answer – there were other "barbarians" throughout the Roman world, including the Picts "allies" - the Scots. So the term also denotes a unique feature to the Picts, something that makes them different to the Scots. The early descriptions of Picts and Scots do not highlight or mention any difference in features or dress, so that would rule this out, and we are ultimately left with one characteristic, that separates the

Picts from other "barbarians" anywhere else in the world – they are native Britons. This makes them different from their "allies", the Scots that came from Ireland – the Romans already knew that – Agricola had entertained an exiled Irish Prince and the archaeology of South West Scotland shows evidence of migration in the 6th century BC – 1st century AD, overlapping with the beginning of the Roman occupation.

So the term Pict indicates that they were a "barbarian, uncivilised native Briton", someone outside of the influences of Roman civilisation. But this term is really what it has come to mean to the Roman and Romano-British viewpoint – to them it is an insult – if you are a Pict you are unworthy of living, you are a violent, bloodthirsty and uncivilised barbarian native of Britain. This explains why Stilicho's troops treat the Picts differently – they have to kill them and subsequently;

"look upon the face of the dying Pict"

The Scientific approach

There is also a scientific approach to working out what the term Pict means. You take some of the key statements e.g. I have selected

- *"hitherto semi-naked Picts and Hbernians"*

- *"Caledoni and other Picts"*

- *"the dying Pict"*

And you ask some key questions – When, Where, What, How and Why, and then look for the common themes

1. What was happening when the statement was made
2. Where is it being made
3. When was something similar said
4. Who has said it
5. Why have they said it
6. How have the said it.

And put together some answers as in the following table

hitherto semi-naked Picts and Hbernians	1. Harassment of Romans invading forces by native Britons and Irish. People threatening and preventing the development of a peaceful, stable civilised Roman society. 2. Britain – (no other location provided) 3. Any alliance – German and Italians, Cowboys and Indians, Apache & Sioux – nations or alliances between large groups of people, not individual small groups 4. Eumenius – Roman writer 5. Propaganda – praising Constantius Chlorus. 6. Written for a Roman educated audience, demonstrating how Constantius Chlorus had subdued an uncivilised people
Caledoni and other Picts	1. Harassment of Roman forces by native Britons and Irish. People threatening and preventing the growth of a peaceful, stable, civilised Roman

society.

2. Britain – again no other location

3. When multiple groups of people share similar characteristics but are in separate groups are mentioned, e.g. kashmiri and other Indians, you, me and other people

4. An unknown Roman writer

5. To praise the Roman Emperor

6. Writing – only a Roman educated audience could read

The dying Pict

1. General Stilicho's army was trying to subdue British rebellion in 4th century AD. A rebellion which threatened the civilised, stable Roman Population

2. Britain – no place-name is mentioned

3. Pro war poems, praising a hero and denigrating their enemies, making their enemies seem cruel and barbaric

4. Another Roman writer for a Roman audience

5. Propaganda again. To show how Stilicho had decimated his non-Roman British opponents.

6. Writing again for a Roman audience

So to summarise the common elements for the term Pict;

1. It's being used by Roman writers, so the word has to make sense to a Roman audience, and identify the carriers of the name as cruel, lawless, bloodthirsty types. A people that the Romans would be glad to see dead.

2. It relates to nationality – like Hibernians – Hibernian are natives of Ireland - Hibernian means Irish, Pict by association within the same phrase must refer to natives of Britain i.e. "British"

3. It relates to people not under the control of Roman Empire. They were opposing Roman "civilisation" – the opposite of civilisation is barbarian.

4. The Picts were human beings, a people, so the term must relate to them being a "people"

5. The Caledoni are a "tribe" of the Picts, so the term "other Picts" must relate to them being divided into tribes

So the conclusion is that Pict refers to them being a British, Barbarian, Tribal People.

The final analysis is to test the hypothesis by replacing the word Pict in the same phrases.

- "hitherto semi-naked Picts and Hbernians" becomes
- hitherto semi-naked Barbarian British tribes

- "Caledoni and other Picts" becomes
- Caledoni and other Barbarian British tribes

- "the dying Pict" becomes

- *The dying British barbarian*

This fits in quite well but could other alternative definitions of Pict make sense.

- *hitherto semi-naked painted people*

bit of a confused sentence – tells us that the Pict used to be semi-naked – then tells us they were painted - then tells us they no longer are semi-naked (so we must assume they are fully dressed, so most of their "painted skin is hidden)"). But then the term is used for the next 600 years. A painted people that don't show off their tattoos?

- *Caledoni and other painted people*

written around 310 when Eumenius has already told us that they used to be semi-naked but are no longer so, and who exactly are the other painted people – there is nothing unique to the practice of tattooing amongst the Picts, the phrase could refer to hundreds of people across the Roman world, in many countries.

- *The dying painted person*

Another meaningless statement – anyone in the Roman Empire could be described as painted, not just someone in Britain

Tattooing was a common Greek or Roman practice to mark slaves and criminals, so to refer to some of the natives as Britain as painted people, ignores the fact that they were "painting people" in their own cities. The Roman word for tattoo was not picti, it was stigma – a word that we still use today in reference to permanent reputational damage caused by either misfortune or misdeed.

It is likely that many of the legionnaires along the Roman wall had a tattoo. The 4th century Roman writer Vegetius described how recruits should only be given the official mark by pin pricks once they had tested themselves in military exercises The "painted people" were therefore present in the Roman army.

The other proposed definition for Pict is that it derives from Pecht – meaning ancestor. A quicker summary of the reworded phrases

- *Hitherto semi-naked ancestors*
- *Caledoni and other ancestors*
- *The dying ancestor*

These make no sense. The Picts weren't anyone's ancestors, they were contemporary with the people writing about them, they were the same age, possibly younger than the people that they were fighting against, and the Romans believed their gods were the only real gods, so there could be no people with any genuine older religious practices. The Picts simply weren't ancestors, they may have been related to other British and Romano-British tribes but as cousins, not their parents, grandparents or great grandparents.

The only phrase that makes sense is that Pict means a British barbarian, and Picts refers to "British Barbarian tribes".

This fits in very well with the Roman testimonies, instead of Pict, we can substitute "barbarian tribes of Britain" into any of the phrases used in Roman testimonies.

Who provided the term

But this is only the Roman view and what the term has come to mean to Romans and the Romano-British. The meaning of the name really lies in who came up with the term first. After all "Benedict Arnold" was really just an individual's name, until the American Wars of Independence started in 1776. After this the name became a byword for treachery and deceit Has something similar occurred with the term Pict.

We have 2 options either the Picts were named by the Romans, (or the Romano-British), or they used an internal name, which the Romans, as they did with many other languages, simply picked up.

The case for a Roman Origin

In support of the former case is the fact that the Picts do not leave us with anything that links them to the name Pict, Their name in Gaelic is Cruithne, or in Irish Gaelic Cruithin. Their tribes appear to fail to contain any reference to the word Pict, and by the 12th century any reference to the name Pict has completely disappeared and everyone more or less tells us that the entire group were extinct, when there is no evidence at all to suggest any ethnic cleansing had taken place that would have eradicated them.

The Romans were not made up of Latin speakers and mainly contained soldiers taken from all parts of the Roman Empire, where multiple languages were being spoken. The Roman army did not exhibit any propensity for renaming groups of people and would often use the differences between tribal groups to play one off against the other in order to "divide and rule" - something they would not be able to do if they were renaming local tribes.

We have examples of the naming of people from recent European history that can provide a reference for this practice. In 1492 when Columbus arrived in the West Indies, he called the natives "Indians", a name that stuck with the native Americans for centuries. This was a new name for them, as they were divided, like the Picts, into different tribes. Columbus did not choose the name though, he used it because he thought he had arrived in India. India is a local name, arising from the old Persian word, Indus, their version of the word Hindus. He called them, what he thought, was a native name. The Romans would have done the same – used what they thought was a local name.

The case for a "Pictish" Origin

I favour this case – maybe it's just a personal preference. To me, it seems more logical for a group that had, in all likelihood coalesced to support each other under one banner, would choose an identity they could all share, and support. The name continues to be used throughout the 5th, 6th, 7th and 8th centuries while the Picts were still in existence, and the Roman Army had long since left.

The reason for the name arising may lie in the Pictish king list. This demonstrates that they were not heterogeneous, and the tribes, like their leadership, were mainly P and Q Celtic.

Ammianus Marcellinus talked of a Barbarian conspiracy, and the merging of several tribes together in this list seems to support the notion that there was an alliance of tribes, mainly in the North. We have evidence of major resistance to the Roman occupation. There was the revolt of the Iceni under Boudica, Queen Cartamandua betrayed and handed over 7 Kings that were resisting Roman Rule, The Emperor Probus brought in barbarian troops from Germany to suppress insurrections, Constantius Chlorus' army was harassed by Picts and Scots, and at one point Nero withdrew his troops due to difficulties of keeping Britain under Roman rule.

Essentially the Roman Empire, their Armies, Governors and Emperor were almost continuously experiencing revolt from many parts of Britain from a combination of tribes, who like the Pictish coalition were a combination of P and Q Celtic speakers, they were in communication with each other and it is to this language that we would look to to find the origin of the name Pict.

The Pictish king list is a list of tribes of Britain, but only some of them – those that resisted the Roman Occupation, such as the Caledoni. These tribes claim descent from the eponymous British ancestor Brude, or as Geoffrey of Monmouth has it Brutus. But while Brude is the father figure, the other ancestor is his "wife" the eponymous An, or Anu. An would in this case, be a "mother goddess"

The Irish legends state that the Picts took their kings from the female line, so it would make sense that it is with An that the Picts look to find their name. An would represent the entire land of Britain and all of the associated tribes present, but the Pictish king list only represents part of the people of Britain.

By tradition the presence of the word Pet is how we identify Pictish place names This word is a derivative of the P Celtic welsh word peth, and literally means a piece or a part. The Picts also included Q Celtic tribes, so the corresponding Gaelic word cuid would be how we define the presence of Q Celtic Pictish place names

The Pictish nation were a hybrid of both P and Q Celtic

tribes in alliance together so in areas where they coalesced together, both words would be present. A truly Pictish place name would have to include references to both words – Peth and Cuid.

The presence of Brude in the Pictish king demonstrates that their allegiances were to the same beliefs as the Britons, so it would make logical sense that their name begins with the P Celtic word – Peth, which means that Cuid would have to follow on from this. Combining both words we get something that sounds roughly as Pethcuit.

In combining these 2 words, the problem we next have is one of emphasis – whether the th sound dominates or the C sound dominates. If the c sound dominates, the th becomes either more like an h, or completely silent – and if anyone listens to the way Scots pronounce Britain colloquially (i.e without the emphasis on using "proper English") the t almost disappears entirely – Britain become Bri'_'an. This may be due to the tendency to speak very quickly or just the accent itself. So with a Scottish accent, Peh'cit becomes Pe'c't and ultimately sounds exactly like Pict. The word Pict, then becomes a combination word, simply meaning part.

This then fits in nicely with the Pictish king list and the Celtic Origin story. Marcellinus told us that the sons of Hercules, gave their names to the territories that they inhabited. The tribes subsequently took their name from these territories. Gildas told us that the Celts worshipped the land and their prominent features, so their names reflected the prominent features of the land.

The land was An, it was subdivided into territories or parts of An, and the People took their name from those parts. The name Pict means a part, the people in each territory identified themselves as a part. Their tribes were Picts. Pict is simply another word meaning tribe – a tribe that occupied a part of An. The Picts were tribes of An that retained their native Celtic traditions - "barbarian tribes". The name Pict is not a people or a race, but signifies a tribe of Britain resisting Roman rule. A Pictish tribe is one part of a group of tribes that inhabited Britain and refused/resisted the change to Roman rule.

Although I favour this "home-grown" argument it is also possible that it may have just come about through sheer "language laziness" - Roman or Native – a tribe is either pet, or cuid depending on the language they spoke, so rather than try and distinguish between the groups they just merged the 2 words together to get Pict. Whatever the reason, the word is straightforward and makes perfect sense, You could substitute the word Picts with the term "Barbarian British tribes" in virtually every statement in the Roman sources make and it makes complete sense.

Each mention of the word Pict that appears in Roman, Dark Age and Medieval sources is unlikely to be about the entire group of tribes within the Pictish coalition. Each individual tribe or group, not under Roman control, can justifiably be called a Pict. In later years this may have extended itself to the notion of adherence to a Christian god, Christianity being a development brought during the Roman Occupation and which was still heavily influenced by the remains of the Roman Empire that had evolved into the early Catholic Church, Any native tribes not Christian can then be called a Pict.

The Brigantes – another Pictish tribe

Eumenius first uses the term "Picts" around 297AD in praise of The Emperor Constantius Chlorus' achievements. And the timing of this is key to naming the principle "Barbarian

British tribe" involved in resisting Roman occupation. In his poem Eumenius writes;

"a nation, still savage and accustomed to the hitherto semi-naked Picts and Hbernians as their enemies, yielded to to Roman Arms and standards without difficulty"

Eumenius gives the impression that the Picts were in existence during the time of Julius Caesar, but Julius Caesar only encountered The Catevellauni in 55 and 54BC around Kent and the Thames Valley – if he had encountered Picts these were the Picts he encountered – they didn't yield to Roman Arms and Standards and continued to resist Roman Advances.

If Eumenius was correct then the tribes that surrendered to the Romans without difficulty were the "nation" and the Picts and Hibernians are the ones that resisted Roman advances and there may be some truth in this.

The Roman invasion began around 43AD. And between then and 297AD the following events occurred where the Roman Army encountered serious resistance to Roman occupation

- Catevellauni & Dumnoni - (Kent, Cornwall & Devon)- 43AD
- Iceni – of Norfolk - former allies of Rome – revolted 47AD
- Catevellauni – under Caratacus – revolted 50AD
- Silures – of Wales – start a guerilla warfare campaign – just as the Picts did in later centuries – 52AD
- Iceni – under Boudica – revolted 61AD
- Brigantes – Northern England – under Venutius overthrow the Roman Collaborator Queen

- Cartamandua and revolt - 69AD
- Caledoni – under Calgacus – fought Roman Army at Battle of Mons Grapius – 83AD
- Pressure from Northern tribes, including Brigantes forces Roman back to Tyne Solway line – between 85-90AD
- Hadrian's wall is built but with many Forts facing south in order to subdue Brigantes in Northern England – 122AD.
- Antonine Wall built c. 160AD to extend Roman frontier into Southern Scotland, had to be abandoned due to revolt of Brigantes – 163AD
- Brigantes and Northern Tribes fight and harass Roman Army around Hadrian's wall for years to come – 163AD (onwards)
- Brigantes and other local tribes revolt around Hadrian's wall - 197AD.
- Guerilla warfare campaign waged by Caledonians leads to peace treaty between Rome and Northern British tribes – Britannia Superior and Britannia minor created – 209AD.

From the above there is one Celtic tribe giving Rome it's biggest headache – the Brigantes – they seem to be at the heart of most of the troubles Rome had been experiencing around their Northern Border. They are inside and outside the Hadrian's Wall region and have been mentioned on 6 separate occasions. They have forced Roman Armies to move their border back on at least 3 separate occasions.

This is many more times than any other tribes. Yet Eumenius doesn't criticise them, doesn't refer to them in his discourse – this can only be because he is including them amongst the term "The Picts", i.e. the British Barbarian tribes, situated right next to "Hibernians" is the Brigantes.

Around 367AD Ammianus Marcellinus talks about the war on the Border region

"But in Britain, during Constantius' tenth and Julian's third year of consulship, the wild tribes of the Scots and the Picts broke their undertaking to keep peace, were causing destruction in those areas near the frontiers, and the provincials, exhausted by the repeated disasters they had already suffered, were caught in the grip of fear"

The Brigantes, were based both inside and outside Hadrian's wall, as shown in the following diagram. Their territories probably extended above the Tweed into lowland Scotland

They fought the Roman Army at every opportunity in the previous years, why wouldn't they seize the opportunity in the 4th century AD, to create more trouble for the Roman Army. Of course they would – The Brigantes are part of the "other" Picts that Marcellinus was talking about.

They were in the perfect location to attack with other "barbarian British tribes". The Modus Operandi shown in their previous history makes them the most likely group to break the peace treaty. The Caledonians live well away from the Roman Border. The Brigantes lived right on top of it. They have a history of frequent revolts and have to be the likeliest people to break the treaty.

The frightened provincials were not the native tribes – Roman writers tend to discount these in their records – they were the people that were there to make their living around Hadrian's wall, providing services to the occupying Roman Army. The Pictish King list was missing at least 6 tribes, one more would not be a surprise and the circle and wave symbols in the Dunnichen stone could then be more balanced.

7 was a Celtic magic number and it makes perfect sense for there to be 7 waves in one circle and 7 in another. One can't help think this may be a 6th-8th century play on words, "waves of people" The Verturiones would now be comprised of the Taezali, the Cornavi, the Caerini, the Smertae, the Selgovae, the Votadini and the Brigantes.

The Seven "Missing" Kingdoms

At the start of the Pictish Chronicle comes the origin tale for the Pictish Kings, Cruithne, son of Cinge, appears to divide the country into 7 territories.

1. Cait, or Cat
2. Ce
3. Circinn
4. Fib
5. Fidach
6. Fotla
7. Fortriu

We think of this as being the following districts;

Caithness & Sutherland, Angus & The Mearns, Mar & Buchan, Fife, Invernesshire, Atholl and Strathearn & Menteith.

But the division of Fib – refers to it being *"a warlike clan"* – so this becomes a division of people, not a division of land and, in that respect, correlates to the series of Brudes. There is an obvious link to the names of some tribes (such as **Fot**la and **Vota**dinia, **Cae**rini and **Ce**) and we can work out the rest from the location of the tribes on Ptolomey's Geographia. The most likely relationship is the following

1. Caerini (Ce)
2. Taezali (Cat)
3. Cornavi (Circinn)
4. Smertae (Fib)
5. Selgovae (Fidach)
6. Votadini (Fotla)
7. (Northern) Brigantes (Fortriu)

With Cal appearing in the series of Brudes. The Brudes have to be the group that Marcellinus refers to as Dicalydones, This makes the 7 "missing" tribes the Verturiones. Of course this also mean that these tribes are not located in the traditional areas that we associate them with, this is likely to be due to the territorial names being assigned much, much later, for example the "kingdom" of Fife was first mentioned in 1678, 600 years or so later than the Pictish Chronicle source material. It may be named after the Fib of the Pictish Chronicle but this looks to have occurred hundreds of years afterwards and with no real evidence of a link between the modern Fife, and the people of Fib.

The Pictish Chronicle does not represent an ancient list of prehistoric kings. It's early part is primarily an account of the native barbarian tribes residing in Britain during the 4th, 5th and 6th centuries AD.

The Brudes of An being preceded by Cruithne and Cinge also fits in with the Celtic Origin story - Brutus was the descendant of Aeneas, who himself was a relic of the Trojan wars, so Aeneas himself had an older ancestry going back all the way to Noah. In the Christian world God exists from the beginning of time but in the ancient world it is quite common for the chief god, to have parents, grandparents and great grandparents. The Greek Gods were children of Chronos (Saturn), Odin was the son of Borr, son of Buri. The Pictish King List appears to fall in line with Celtic and North European beliefs..

The Scots Tribes

As the Pictish Chronicle, or at least the beginning of it, is a list of tribes, we can also identify the name and location of the Scots tribes. The indications are that the Picts were divided into 2 groups of 7 tribes each – in accordance with Celtic beliefs – Under the sons of Cruithne are 7 tribes, and under the Father of the sons of An (Brude ap Ant) are 13 names. So the names of the "ancestor" start the sequence of tribal lists. According to Bede, the ancestor of the Scots was **Ru**eda so logically **Ru** starts the sequence of Scots tribes

Brude Ru   *Brude Urru*
Brude Gart   *Brude Urgart*
Brude Cinid   *Brude Urcinid*
Brude Uip   *Brude Uruip*
Brude Grid   *Brude Urgrid*
Brude Mund   *Brude Urmund*

The Scots tribes are therefore Gart, Cinid, Uip, Grid and Mund. These would be as follows;

- Gart - the Carnonacae.

- Cinid – A North Wales tribe, Irish tribes did not just settle in Scotland. The Deisi were an Irish tribe that settled in North Wales. They settled in Gwynedd, and in the 3rd or 4th century the warrior Cunedda was brought in from North Britain to force them to withdraw back to Ireland, The Cinid are the Scots tribe that settled in North Wales, Cunedda and Gwynedd is a corruption of the same name.

- Uip - the Epidi.

- Grid - the Credones.

- Mund - the Dumnoni of Strathclyde (and connected with the inhabitants of Munster, the original home of the Dal Riada).

The Senchus Fer'n Alban, tells us their were 6 brothers that settled in Scotland, and one left behind in Ireland. So although only 5 groups are listed in the Chronicle, the Senchus provides us with 7 groups - the magical no. 7 again.

Adjusting the Pictish Chronicle

The Pictish Chronicle begins with Cinge, a word that is simply a variant of the "Saxon" word Cyn and the Gaelic Ceann, both meaning King or Chief. So it is also about the structure of the way the "Picts" are governed – probably with an Over-King.

In the word Verturiones, we can see the name Cruithne appearing (with only a slight manipulation of C and V sound which can be interchangeable – this is often the reasoning in other historical works, where the "Goddodin" of Aineirin's poem, are linked directly to the Votadini). This makes the 7 "Sons of An" the DiCalydones, and the 5 "sons of Ru" are the Scots.

We can now draw up a table, assigning the tribes to the correct group.

Sons of Cruithne (Verturiones)	Sons of An (Dicalydones)	Sons of Ru (Dal Riada - Scots)
Caerini	Lugi	Epidi
Taezali	Canti (Decantae)	Dumnoni
Cornavi	Caledoni	Carnonacae
Smertae	Novantae	Credones
Selgovae	Venicones	Cinidones ? - the Deisi of Wales
Votadini	Vacomagi	
Brigantes	Cintiaci	

A number of these tribes are not in the same geographical area. This is not uncommon or unusual – Migrating ethnic peoples of the 17th, 18th, 19th and 20th Centuries such as Jewish, Irish, Italian, French, African, Asian etc. spread out and formed local communities in many different locations, countries, towns and cities - we only have to think of the Welsh speaking communities of the Argentine Patagonia for evidence of this.

It is only to be expected that earlier migrating peoples arriving over several centuries would do the same. Between the 5th and 8th centuries AD Ogham inscriptions appeared in Ireland, Scotland, Wales, the Isle of Man, and England in Hampshire, Cornwall and Devon, There are Gaelic influences found in the placenames and words of Cumbria, as well as Brythonic "Welsh", confirming settlements of "Irish" people were being made in these areas. One thing we can say though is that the table provides evidence that the Cruithne (or Cruithin) are Picts, but not all Picts are Cruithne, and strangely enough we now have 3 distinct groups which we can separate ;

1. Cruithne – the Cruithin of Irish legend. The Picts – was it their language Bede referred to – a mix of Scandinavian and Welsh, or the "Cornish" language of South West England.
2. The Dicalydones – the "Britons" using Welsh style placenames such as Aberdeen, and welsh style gods – llew (Lugi) etc.
3. The Dal Riada – the Scots

It is likely that other names are hidden in the Pictish king list Drest, Breide, Nechtan were not intended as names in the modern sense. They are descriptive terms, for example the word Drest contains the Norse word Hest, meaning horse, which links to the Gaelic word Each, for Horse and ultimately to the Epidi of Argyll - a "horse" tribe. This link to a "horse" is also found in the name of several early Scottish Kings such as Eochaid, Eachdach etc. while the horse symbol is displayed on one of the surviving fragments of a class 1 Pictish Stone in Inverurie, Aberdeenshire.

Chapter 9: The Epidi – a lost Pictish/Scottish tribe

The Epidi have a very curious position in relation to the Picts. The Epidi are known to share a prehistoric common culture with the Irish of Northern Ireland, evidence of this can be found in the rock carvings of both Ulster and Argyll, yet there is no evidence of any settlement from Ireland in later years, so they do not appear to be Scots either. There is also the question of the Boar symbol that appears in the ancient hill fort thought to be Dunadd. The Boar symbol is supposed to represent the Pictish Royal family.

It is highly likely that the Epidi were distantly related to the ancient Irish inhabitants of Ulster, and thereby the Scots of Southern Scotland, but they were also likely to be related to their northern and eastern neighbours as well – they are in the perfect location to mix with the Picts of Northern Scotland and the Irish of Ulster and Southern Scotland.

Is it possible that they they were a combination tribe. In the Roman period, other than the Caledonians, we do not have a single tribe, named in the Pictish King List, that we can be link to the Pictish group. The Pictish king list is a medieval document thought to date back to a 10th century source and as such is not contemporary with this period of time.

The Picts and the Scots shared similar characteristics, at least in legend, the Scots were a mixture of Picts and Irish, and the Picts, strangely enough were also a mixture of Picts and Irish. In legend they both originate from Ireland and settle in North Britain, close to each other. We know that the Scots were living close to the Epidi, both not far from the northern Irish coast, is it possible that the Epidi have contributed to these legends of Pictish/Irish relationships were the Epidi, of Argyll, Picts, Scots or a mixture of both.

The Epidi are in a unique position, they have Scots below them and Picts to the side of them, There is also another tribe with a similar sounding name on the islands opposite them – the Ebudae. With such a close relationship between them we have to consider whether the Epidi are a "true" Pictish group – or are they a hybrid – do they fit into both camps. Are they in fact the result of the mixing of Picts to the East and North of them and Scots and Irish to the West and South of them.

The ancestor of the Epidi appears in the Pictish king list as Uip – missing the pid or pet ending. Pet is a welsh word and we can see it in Pictish place-names Through the use of the word Pet, The Epidi would have to be defined as "Irish" Picts and they would be the first ones to demonstrate the use of the term. They are also likely to provide the inspiration for the legends of the Picts being mixed with the Irish – being centrally located between both groups.

The fortress in Argyll, that we believe is called Dunadd, must now be seen as a Pictish fort, but with an allegiance to the Scots. This would explain the carving of what may be the boar symbol - a symbol associated with Pictish kings - that may be seen there.

Chapter 10: The evolution of Roman-Britain

Around 49AD, something occurred which would change the way the Romans saw the British. They established a base at Colchester for their Roman Legions. But when the legionnaires left around 69-79AD, the base became a colonia – A Roman colony where their former soldiers would live, work, raise families, i.e. where former Romans could become citizens of a Roman Britain, thus we get a new group in Britain, something we have never considered before – Romano-British.

Around 79AD the Romans encouraged the citizens of Britain to adopt Roman culture, their former soldiers of Britain settling into civitas, either new towns and villages or ones that were transformed from the old "barbarian" ways.

Around 150AD the Romano-British, a people descended from both former soldiers of the Roman Empire that had settled into Britain, and from those barbarian tribes that had adopted the new way of life, start to build Roman style Villas and Buildings across the country.

But not all of Britain was under Roman Control – we need to stop thinking of Hadrian's Wall as the boundary wall between Roman-Britain and Barbarian Britain. This was an incoming army trying to control a barbarian society, that was spread out wide across all of the land. The Romans built 8000 miles of roads, many new cities, settlements, army camps and forts, but this was really the ancient equivalent of the "Wild West". The Roman Army could only control those areas that they were able to get to quickly, those areas that they could cover by foot. They could not get to the remote rural areas. Like the later American West the army could not control the "badlands" - the places that they couldn't see, the mountain areas of Wales, the

Pennines, the Lake District. The places farthest away from their power centres. They needed "alliances" with "friendly tribes" to retain control, but those tribes were still for the most part native. They were Picts

Around 367AD Ammianus Marcellinus talks of Picts and Scots attacking frontiers in plural. Britain did not have just one solitary Northern Frontier, it had many frontiers. Unlike the Soldiers of the U.S. Cavalry, the Romans did not have a massive technological advantage. Yes they had some vicious weapons that were very effective attacking the natives when they were all gathered at one location, such as Maiden castle in Dorset. But in areas where the natives were strung out, hidden amongst trees, bushes, rocks and in the undergrowth, moving rapidly from one place to another, they had very little advantage, if any. The natives of Britain had iron age weapons – sharp, strong metal swords, axes, spears, and not stone axes like the native Americans. The Romans had similar weaponry, not the rifles, shotguns and pistols of the U.S. Cavalry. Away from their bases, on uneven ground, travelling slowly, in a country that they did not know, the Roman soldier had very little advantage

So in Roman Britain we have a native population, worshipping old gods and sticking to older native practices, living in the outer regions – the frontiers of Britain – the wild lands across Scotland, England and Wales, that the Roman Army could only occasionally reach, and where they would meet with little success – this is the land of the Picts to the Romans. The Romano-British the "civilised" citizens that lived in the towns and cities, that grew up along the roads and trading routes that the Roman Army established, and the Roman Army and it's followers – the retainers, servants and dependants, drawn from all over the Roman Empire that served it's needs and lived in permanent, semipermanent and temporary housing near the forts and camps, that they relied on.

The Changing nature of the Romano-British

There is a tendency to believe that the Romano-British were subservient, grateful even to the Roman Empire, and remained true to the Government in Rome. In fact there is very good evidence to suggest that there was a growing sense of "Britishness" developing amongst the new "Romano-British". and that there was a desire to cede the country away from Rome

It is in the 3rd century AD, c. 259 AD, Britain, Spain and Gaul were dramatically separated from the rest of the Roman Empire. The general Postumus had seized control and made himself Emperor of the Gallic Empire. This lasted for the next 15 years. Thus almost a full generation grew up in which the Romano-British no longer owed allegiance or paid homage to the Caesar in Rome, His Consuls or Government.

In 274 AD the Gallic Empire was re-absorbed by the Roman Empire, but just 13 years later in 287AD, Carasius, the admiral of the Empire's channel fleet, declared himself Emperor of Britain and Northern Gaul. His successor and probable murderer Allectus, reinforced the defences on the Saxon Shore – which was principally to defend his "Empire" from the pending invasion by the main Roman Army, which eventually came around 296AD. Allectus eventually died in a battle near Silchester.

It seems incredible to believe that this drive for separation was not supported by the Romano-British. As the 6th century historian Procopius states during the reign of Constantius

"And the island of Britain revolted from the Romans……. However the Romans never succeeded in recovering Britain, but it remained from that time on under tyrants"

This is more than a hint that Britain had reached an independent state, and that Britain was no longer being controlled by Rome. This is the evidence that the Romano-British had found a desire for self determination, and saw themselves as belonging to Britain rather than Rome. The Romano-British now saw themselves as Britons. This is not unusual. There are examples of this in our own recent and not so recent history.

After the Norman Conquest of Ireland, Anglo-Norman Lords settled there, but by 1366, the statutes of Kilkenny complained that they;

"live and govern themselves according to the manners, fashion, and language of the Irish enemies"

The Tudors also tried to supplant the native inhabitants of Ireland with English colonists, but by the seventeenth century a similar complaint was made that they were

"more Irish than the Irish"

We see this same behaviour in Georgian times, in the British colonies when the Americans found a new sense of identity and broke free of British control.

<u>The new Roman Britain</u>

By the 4th century AD, there was a new sense of identity in Britain, and amongst that we can now see various groups clearly emerging.

1. The Romano-British

A mixed group - They have taken on the traditions, customs and practices belonging to Rome, but have found a sense of Britishness. They identify themselves as Britons and have some ancestry that traces them back to the original native inhabitants, and they claim this as a birthright. They wish for independence from Rome, but are afraid of any change in their lifestyle or government. The Roman Army, Picts and Scots are all their immediate threat.

2. The Picts

These are the genuine native inhabitants of Britain – they don't have the customs, practices and traditions of Rome and adhere to the older native traditions of Britain. They are found in the remoter parts of Britain – the frontier lands, the edges of the Roman Britain that cannot be reached or are too wild for the Roman Army to control. There will be some mixed marriages but their traditions remain mainly as they were before the Roman Invasion. They frequently harass the Roman Army and mount guerilla warfare campaigns against them where they can use their weapons, knowledge of the country to their advantage. They wish for a return to the old ways, The Roman Army and the Romano-British are their enemy.

3. The Scots

The later settlers from Ireland that arrived in South West Scotland in the 1st century AD, may have been encouraged by the Roman General Agricola – Tacitus mentions that he entertained an exiled Irish Prince around the Nithsdale region. The story of the settlement of the Dal Riada in Britain appears to mirror this event as Caibre Riata, was exiled from Ireland and sought refuge in Britain, where he founded the second colony of Dal Riada.

The Saxon

We could not mention the people of Britain without mentioning the Saxons. Although the Roman writers testify to the presence of the Saxons raiding and harassing Britain and Northern Europe in the late 4th and 5th centuries AD, the statistics that I provided in my earlier work "The History of the Scots, Picts and Britons" demonstrated that it would have been almost impossible for these later Saxons to have settled Britain in the no.s required for the DNA results produced. It is from the words of Gildas when he relates that, after the Rescript of Honorius, to aid the Britons against the barbarians;

"Then all the members of the council, together with the proud tyrant, were struck blind; the guard - or rather the method of destruction - they devised for our land was that the ferocious Saxon (name not be spoken), hated by man and God should be let into the island like wolves into the fold, to beat back the peoples of the north... Of their own free will they invited under the same roof a people whom they feared worse than death even in their absence"

In actual fact we get a different story from the 5th century Greek historian Zosimus when he tells us that during the reign of the Emperor Probus in the 3rd century

He[Probus] made war on the Burgundi and the Vandili. But seeing that his forces were too weak, he endeavoured to separate those of his enemies, and engage only with a part….the Romans challenged the Barbarians that were on the further side to fight….and fought until the Barbarians were all either slain or taken by the Romans……All of them that were taken alive were sent to Britain, where they settled, and were subsequently very serviceable to the emperor when any insurrection broke out".

The German barbarians arrived in Britain in the 3rd century AD which is when we see archaeological evidence in the South East of the migration of Germanic people into Britain. The remains of Germanic soldiers in the Roman Army have been found in Britain, which seems to confirm Zosimus' statement. There is no evidence of any later settlement.

We may also see evidence in Ptolomey's' map of earlier Germanic settlement in the names of North European tribes such as the Canti, the Atrebate, the Regni and the Belgae, and we must not forget that the name of the tribe from whom England takes it's name the **Angli,** is contained in the tribe of the name Dec**angli**.

Chapter 11: The Evolution of the Picts

The Picts were the native British tribes of Britain. The name develops between the 1st and 3rd centuries AD, probably after 49AD when the first Roman Colony settles in Colchester, and over the new few centuries, it evolved to mean many things to many people. It evolves as follows;

Prehistory

Britain and Ireland are being settled by many different groups from c. 5000BC onwards. These groups come from various places – Iberia (Spain & Portugal), Gaul (France & Belgium), Germania (Germany & Austria, Hungary etc.), Scythia (Scandinavia, Orkneys, Shetland &, Russia), Ireland. Further internal movements occur and several groups find branches in different parts of the British Isles, such as the Brigantes (Southern Scotland, Northumberland, Yorkshire, Ireland), Dumnoni (Devon, Ireland, Scotland), Cornavi (Cornwall, Northern Scotland) etc. There is not one language spoken in Britain, there are many languages being spoken. The last invasion from Europe was by La Tene era Celts from "Beyond the Rhine". Continuous cross border settlement between Ireland and North Britain occurred on the South West Coast of Scotland until the Roman Occupation. The distribution of people is sporadic and mixed, small pockets of unrelated groups of older and newer populations speaking different languages exist within many regions.

1st - 4th Centuries AD.

The Picts appear in this period, probably using the term to define themselves as native, i.e. non-Roman "British" tribes. They were generally a mix of P Celtic and Q Celtic speaking tribes, with perhaps some ancient Scandinavian thrown in,

The name develops, probably organically, as a way of differentiating themselves from the new tribes in Britain, which were;

The Scots

Incoming tribes from Ireland, that first started arriving around the 6th century BC, and some of whom were probably encouraged to settle in later times by the Romans as a way of controlling the British tribes in those regions that they could not get to, and later went "native" seizing the opportunity to add to their wealth and territory as the Roman Empire started to weaken

The Romano-British

The new tribes in Britain, the settlers that mixed with the local population and created the Roman towns and cities, and raised families. These people then evolved and became "more British than the Britons". They then claimed an ancient British ancestry, though this was only a portion of their make-up As they became more ardent in opposing "Roman rule", the more rebellious may well have taken up arms and become the mysterious Attacoti, mentioned by Ammianus Marcellinus.

The Saxons

Germanic tribes in the South, some arriving in the period before the Roman invasion, later groups joining them to assist the Romans in keeping the rebelling Britons under control

As far as the Romans were concerned the Pict was any native British tribe that was "uncivilised". The Brigantes in the North, Silures in Wales were Picts as much as the

Caledonians. Hence the Picts are always the ones causing trouble in the "frontiers" of Britain.

When the Romans left, it was the Romano-British that may have appealed to Honorius, it was not the native British.

5th Century AD

When the Romans left, the Picts took on a new identity, that of untrustworthy, violent irreligious (apostate) slave traders, kidnappers and abusers of innocent Christians, thanks to the words of St Patrick.

St Patrick was a Romano-Briton, the son of a priest, grandson of a deacon. He follows the tradition of the Romans and blames, or highlights their brutality and cruelty, of course he fails to mention that slave trading was, at the very least tolerated, and sometimes encouraged by the early Christian church. Even in the fifth century slave trading was being practised throughout the Christian world, including the remains of the - now Christian - Roman empire.

We now see the Picts evolving as opponents and enemies of Christianity – the "Bad Guys".

6th century AD

In the sixth century the Picts get defined even further, but by another native Romano-British (or at least Romano-British educated) monk – Gildas.

For the first time we get the impression of an entirely northern origin, when he says

"she [Britain] groaned aghast for many years, trodden

underfoot first by two exceedingly savage overseas nations , the Scots from the north west and the Picts from the North..".

This is the phrase that develops 2 legends in the minds of monks like Bede and Nennius. Gildas described Britain as 800 miles long in the opening paragraph of the De Excidio Britonnium and then followed it up with this phrase. This is when the legend of the Orkney and Scythian origin begins.. Britain, from the tip of the North of Scotland, to the far edges of the South of England is 800 miles long, so the Picts came from the Northern regions beyond these points, north of the edges of Britain lies the Orkney Islands, and the semi-mythical land of Scythia.

The early medieval monks concluded overseas meant north, outside the land of Britain, above Scotland, and therefore in the land of the Orkneys. Strangely enough no-one questioned the Scots origins - Ireland lies directly to West of Britain and they just needed to sail directly East from Ireland. Mind you Gildas was a Saint and obviously Saint's can't be wrong.

Gildas probably didn't mean they came from overseas – more that their culture was foreign to Britain, or rather foreign to the Romano-British, who saw their Roman style culture as the ancient "British", including the official religion of the latter Roman Empire, Christianity.

From the words of Gildas evolved the notion of a later "Pictish" arrival, coming from the Northern Lands above Britain. The Orkneys and Scythia.

7th Century AD

In the seventh century AD, thanks to Adomnan we think we

can locate the Pictish capital in Inverness, The local tribes of Picts worshipping the Loch Ness monster whom Columba calms through the power of his divinity, and during the course of his visit curing the druid Briochan with a "magic pebble". But Adomnan was a politician and opportunist, he had a reason for writing the tale of Columba, which lay in the political differences in the early churches and not in the divinity of the founder of Iona.

Inverness doesn't figure until the late Victorian/Early 20th century, when the legend of the Loch Ness monster first appeared around 1871 – approximately 1300 years later than Adomnan's tale. The water beast of the River Ness that Adomnan talked about became associated with the legend of the Loch Ness monster and that is when the legend of Columba calming down the Loch Ness monster surfaces, and because of the proximity, Breide Mac Maelcon's fortress becomes the ancient hill fort on Inverness.

There is no way to link the Pictish capital to any place anywhere.

8th Century AD

In the eighth century we find the monk Bede writing his Ecclesiastical History, and now we get the stories that we recognise as uniquely Pictish. We hear of the Scythian origin, the matrilineal succession, the defeats and victories at the hands of the Northumbrians.

The Scythian origin is a misinterpretation of the words of Gildas. Like Gildas, he fails to recognise the development of the Romano-British, during the Roman occupation, and that their claims of "British" descent are only partially accurate.

The matrilineal succession has some basis in fact, however, we have the sons of Erc – the "mother" of Muiredach Mac Erc, an early High King of Ireland, as a possible source of the Erb name in the Pictish King List, and the Senchus Fer 'n' Alban states that

"Two sons of Eochaid Muin-remor, namely Erc and Olchu. And Erc had twelve sons, six of them took possession of Scotland".

There is evidence that the sons of the "mother" figure Erc did become Kings of the Picts. The reigns of the MacErc Kings of Scots, do correspond with the reigns of the Pictish Kings, and this suggests that there was a much earlier take over of Northern Britain by the Scots

Pictish King List	**Dalriadic Monarchs**
Drust (d 478)	Fergus (501? 3 year reign)
Talore (478-482)	Angus Mor?
Nechtan (482-506)	Domangart Ness' son (d 506)
Drest Gurthinmoch (506-36)	Comgall (506-537)
Drust son of Gyrom (536-558)	Gabran (d 559)
Brude Mac Maelcon (558-584)	Conall (559-)

My own belief however is that the "mother" story is a way to explain the succession pattern, Bede came from a society, and by that I mean his religious order, which believed a son succeeds a father, this does not happen in the Pictish King List

The matrilineal succession idea provides a method to explain the Irish claim to the Pictish "throne" and the disorderly way the Pictish society seems to elect it's kings.

Matrilineal succession may be used in times of crisis if a

suitable claimant could not be found. But a claimant from a female line may be more difficult to find than from a male line. Female lives were much shorter than male lives, childbirth was a very dangerous process due to the risk of infection, bleeding so there was a high mortality rate for both child and mother. It would be a huge risk to follow a matrilineal system entirely.

The method of succession was related to the fact that the Picts were a coalition of tribes rather than one group. The choice of ruler was probably elective and wide ranging, from a number of individuals, normally with a familial relationship but not necessarily father to son, or indeed mother to son. It makes it difficult to identify exactly how they succeed, so for a society like Bede's, where succession is parent to child, the logical answer is that it must be due to mother to son, which is why brother succeeds brother, cousin succeeds cousin and nephew succeeds uncle etc.

Bede may well also just have been party to a myth based on a play in words, in the names of some early Pictish King – the Breide's, and the 28 Brude's etc. The name Breide is actually derived from the name Brude, but in Gaelic the word for a bride is bride, and the Norwegian word for Bride is Brud - instead of reading Breide Mac Maelcon, he has followed his own statement and looked at a Scandinavian origin – reading the 28 Brudes and the Breides as the word Bride. To him Breide Mac Maelcon was the Bride of the son of Maelcon – hence the legend of a matrilineal succession begins.

In some cases there was probably not any familial relationship at all. It may be exactly as it was for William the Conqueror, and quite simply a case of strongest man grabbing the crown, and the familial relationship added later.

We always trust Bede's early history for the Kings of the Saxon tribes, but the archaeological evidence suggest otherwise, in most cases we see continuity of settlement rather than conquest and war. Quite likely is that many of the early kings, including those of the Scots, Angles, Britons, Jutes and Saxons had no relationship to each other at all and just "grabbed" the crown, at the first opportunity.

When we reach properly documented history, we find that medieval families struggled to retain the crown for more than a couple of generations before it passed through the female line to another family. It would be unrealistic to expect people living in even more turbulent times to manage to retain the crown in the same family for any more that 2/3 generations either. It just isn't very likely at all.

When the Caesar's obtained possession of the Empire, They knew patrilineal succession was a problem so they created a very unique way of dealing with it. They simply invented a new way. They "adopted" children – Octavian was the nephew of Julius Caesar, but he was "adopted" and became his son. We then see the same practices with nephews, son-in-laws, even individuals with only a token distant relationship. The chances are that most of the ancient genealogies of the monarchies of Scots, Picts, Saxons, etc. are all completely false – even fictitious - something that we don't really challenge as we should.

The matrilineal Pict was a shorthand way to explain a succession pattern that didn't appear to make any sense.

The 9th century

This is the century in which Nennius documents the arrival

of Picts into Britain from Orkney in the pre-Roman period, again a misinterpretation of Gildas and a failure to recognise that the Romano-British were the new development, not the Picts, and mixes the arrival of Picts with La Tene era Celts

It is also the century in which he documents the arrival of "King Arthur" and the linking of Picts, Scots and Saxons in alliance with each other, mimicking the statements by Ammianus Marcellinus of a "barbarian" conspiracy. But Nennius' statement does give us a clue that there were Southern Picts and Scots The Saxons were based in the South East, and yet according to Nennius they were in alliance with the Scots, Picts and harassing the Romano-British tribes in the south. The Pictish king list does show Scots in Wales, and there is archaeological evidence for them in Gwynedd, It also names a Southern tribe within the Romano-Britsh territory. So it would be possible for the Saxons, Scots and Picts to form an alliance within the territories of the Romano-British.

Nennius reinforces the idea of the Romano-British as the ancient British and the Picts as the later incomers. He reinforces the ideas of the Picts, Scots and Saxons as the "bad guys" stealing "British" territory from the rightful inhabitants. This becomes fixed in the minds of medieval historians. In England, the Saxons are the good guys, succeeding to British territory through their warrior like ability – they can't be former "servants" of the Roman Army because that would demean their status – they have to be their "successors".

In Scotland, it is the century which sees the Pictish race extinguished. By the end of the century there were no Kings of Picts left. The Gallowegian King, Kenneth McAlpin may have overthrown the 7 kings of the Pictish kingdoms through a brutal and violent act. But it probably only occurred in the mind of medieval historians as the 7 mormaers of Scotland were still in place until around 1130AD, when David I anglicised the structure of Scottish government and nobility.

Was Kenneth McAlpin a Pict. The simple answer is no, he was, as claimed a Scot from Galloway. The name Alpin that is often referred to as a "Pictish" name is in fact a derivation of the Gaelic and Irish word for Scotland – Alban. It took from 843AD to 900AD to change from being a King of Picts to a King of Alba simply because it required the passing on of the "update" to the scholars of the Celtic world – this was not an overnight process. It doesn't happen that quickly today where many people still use old colonial names for Mumbai (Bombay), Kolcotta (Calcutta) etc.

In truth the Scottish influence had been present well before 500AD when the Scots of the South West grabbed hold of the Pictish crown. Stones are raised and inscribed based on earlier Scandinavian practices, in order to communicate the changes to the more distant populations, or the ones that they had trouble speaking to, because of a difference in language, accent and culture.

Perhaps we should really thank Adomnan et al, for the change, The crucial difference in culture was that the new "Scots" were subject to Celtic church practices of Mungo, Columba etc. while the Gallic Church practices had been abandoned . The "Irish" Celtic church probably played a part in persuading the local communities of the North and North East, that they were in fact of "Irish" descent – Scots. The communities are re-educated, through the "power of prayer" and by the 9th century, they speak the same language, worship the same God, so there is no longer any need to construct the Pictish Stone monuments. Hence St

Columba is the first patron saint of Scotland and not St. Andrew.

By the time we get to the reign of Kenneth McAlpn c. 843AD, it is pretty much ingrained into the population. No communities have changed any names, no violence has been inflicted on them during the course of the change, their homes are in the same places, they work in the same fields, their friends, families are the same people, have the same names etc. so there is absolutely no impact and no-one notices.

By the end of the 9th Century, there is no longer any need to call anyone a "Pict", there are simply no British Barbarians left, everyone is a "civilised" Christian believer. So whether it was Roman, Romano-British or Native, it doesn't really matter - the term has no meaning left. The "Picts" were always someone else – the old "bad guys"

10th century

The first reference to a King of Alba c. 900AD and the Picts are gone for good. The Gaelic name Alba becomes pre-eminent and the term of choice for describing North Britain.

The first Pictish King List is written, combining a mix of ancient legends and religious practices from several different unrelated groups and into a series of mysterious kings going back thousands of years emerges. It's a bit of a mess really, ancient Gods, confused with ancient tribal names, confused with a mix of real and legendary figures, and made up familial links - Nothing different here to the Scots Chronicles, Irish Annals, Bede's Ecclesiastical History or the later Anglo-Saxon Chronicles.

Settlement of the Vikings begins in Britain, Norse languages get spoken in Britain for a while before disappearing, these get confused in later centuries with Bede's statement regarding the Language of the Pict.

11th century

This is the period that the new name for North Britain appears – in Latin form Scotia, in English, Scotland, Crucially it only appears after the South West sub kingdom of Strathclyde merges fully into the North British Kingdom and gains political control of the region. Scotland only becomes Scotland after the South takes charge. The South brought the name Scotland.

It occurs after Malcolm Canmore defeats and kills the usurper Macbeth, The 11st century writer, Simeon of Durham, was absolutely correct in his description of him - Malcolm Canmore was the son of a "king of Strathclyde". Southern influences now reign in Scotland. Edinburgh eventually takes over as a Scottish capital - Southern Scottish practices take hold – Southern Scotland is where the Scots came from and the Scots are now truly in control of government.

The name Scotia comes from a full union of all of the "Irish" descended peoples of North Britain, the Picts, the Gaels and the Scots. This was the point of the legend of the "Egyptian" Princess Scota and Goidel. A merger of the Scots and Gaels as one people, A merger of the last semi-independent Scots sub-kingdom of Strathclyde with the rest of North Britain. The book is now firmly closed on the Picts.

12th Century

Henry of Huntingdon talks of the complete extinction of the Pict, their people, language and customs. Stories emerge now of dark haired Picts, small in stature and emerging from underground homes amongst the Norwegians, and then the Scots. The Picts are starting to be seen as a "past" people – dwarf like, evil and otherworldly. A race very different to the people of Scotland.

Late medieval, Tudor and Stuart periods,

In 1492, the new world was discovered, stories start to arrive of a strange new naked tribal people in the Americas. These stories start to influence the image of the Pict. The Pict is "rediscovered", but as the British equivalent of the native American, The Pict becomes Britain's "noble savage" They are drawn and treated as such – and we start to think of them as a mystical, indigenous, ancient people like the native Americans.

At the end of the Tudor period, there is a crisis, England needs a protestant successor to Elizabeth, the only protestant candidate is James VI of Scotland. This would mean uniting the 2 kingdoms under one king, there is some resistance both in England and Scotland – ancient liberties are at stake. Some historical evidence of a "successful" union is needed, and a link to the ancient Welsh monarchs connecting Stewart origins to those of the Tudors, to ease the union of the crowns of the ancient kingdoms of Scotland and England. The evidence provided – the creation of Anglo-Saxon England, Alfred the Great et al. In Scotland the union of Picts, Britons with Scots – several kingdoms ruled by one king.

Elizabeth's 1st cousin, 2 times removed (not as is often reported her nephew), King James VI of Scotland became her successor, James I of England and promptly up and left Edinburgh for London, taking his wife and children, and his entourage and never returned to Scotland. The Lords and

Ladies of Scotland soon followed, taking some of their wealth with them, to find a place at the "English court". The Picts remain largely anonymous and much as they were seen in the late medieval period but a change was coming - a change that would again dramatically alter how the Picts are viewed.

After a plantation (of Ulster), a rebellion (Cromwell), a dalliance with Puritanism, a monarch's beheading (Charles I), a restoration (Charles II), a religious feud (the Covenanters), a "Glorious Revolution" (James II deposed and succeeded by his daughter Mary, and her Dutch husband William) and the Stuarts Monarchs were ready to oversee the most dramatic change in Scotland and England's history, the Act of Union

17th & 18th Century

In 1690 the Darien Scheme failed – this was an attempt by Scotland to become a world trading colony, and it backfired badly. With almost 20% of the wealth of Scotland lost as a result, Scotland faced a financially bleak future, Among the hierarchy this accelerated the decision to form a political union with England.

This was not a natural decision for the Scots. The 13th & 14th century Wars of Independence, the theft of the Stone of Destiny by Edward I, the "Rough Wooing" by Henry VIII were just a few examples of the problems England had brought to Scotland. The Scots were not going to be happy uniting with their "Auld Enemy" and so it proved.

It was not just the Scots that were unhappy with the 1707 Act of Union either. When a union of parliaments was first proposed almost 100 years earlier by King James VI and I, the parliament of England opposed it because of concerns it would lose it's "ancient liberties". Under the 1705 proposal, the English parliament was even more concerned over the prospect of taking on massive economic liabilities due to the poor state of Scotland's economy and infrastructure.

In Scotland the proposal was violently unpopular. There were riots in Edinburgh. Glasgow and many towns and villages throughout the country. As a result the government issued edicts and threats to the population, warning of dire consequences should they take part or encourage others to participate in the demonstrations. This discontent did not disappear easily, the initial anger and violence subsided, soon afterwards but the resentment remained bubbling under the surface, even after the 1715 and 1745 Jacobite rebellion. In 1791 the bard himself, Robert Burns, reflecting the mood of the people of Scotland decried those that signed the Act of Union agreement as

"Sic a parcel of Rogues in a Nation."

In addition the Scots were witnesses to the frequent attempts to "get rid" of Scotland throughout the 18th and into the 19th century. Although Scotland retained it's own legal system, currency and Presbyterian national church, it was very much a second class citizen, English representation was in the majority in the Westminster Parliament so it had little or no say in the political decisions of the time. The Scots Lords that would have had a political voice had "gone South", sending their children to English Schools to be educated – even today you are, probably, far more likely to find a needle in a haystack, than a hereditary Scots Peer with a genuine Scottish accent. In various maps the name Scotland was replaced by the term North Britain. As early as 1707, not long after the Act was passed, the Royal Scots Greys were renamed the North British Dragoons.

The hierarchy had simply planned for Scotland to cease to exist, it was to become a region called North Britain. The problem was the masses, and mainly those that lived in the South of Scotland, clung on to Scotland.

For the English, the Scots had caused major problems during the 18th century, with 1715 and 1745 Jacobite rebellions. In ignorance of the fact that many Scots had fought on the Hanoverian side rather than side with the Stuarts, in the musical halls of London a new verse had been added to the National Anthem, promising

"Rebellious Scots to crush"

If Scotland was to fully integrate into the new United Kingdom of Great Britain, the Scots needed a new story, they needed to be re-educated, and the English needed to be brought on board to accept them.

Whether consciously or subconsciously, (and to be fair it was probably the latter, combined with the fashion of the time), The Pict also played a part in the revision of Scots History, for a more palatable version.

The 19th & 20th Century

Towards the end of the 18th century, the threat posed by Jacobite rebellions started to fade from memory and the former enemies became looked upon as brave, loyal but misguided figures of romance, This led to the repeal in 1782 of the 1746 act banning Highland Dress and Gaelic traditions. A new fashion began amongst the upper classes and the "great and the good" of society for all things "Scottish", even if it was fictitious.

Opportunists took advantage of this new trend as early as

1760. This was the year James MacPherson published the first of his Ossian Cycle of epic poetry. A series of work that purported to be from authentic Gaelic tales found in the Highlands of Scotland, dating to the 3rd century AD, authored by Ossian, the famous bard of the Irish Fiana, and son of the hero Finn McCool, They were forgeries, but popular and built him an international reputation. Serious scholars challenged and discredited the work almost as soon as it was published, but to many influential people, like the writer John Home, it was a notable work. It helped forge the link between the Highlanders of Scotland and the ancient Irish. No-one pointed out that Finn McCool was primarily a southern Irish hero, viewed in the North as a "racketeer". The early Scots originated from the North of Ireland, where the hero was Cú Chulainn, champion of the Ulaid, whose enemy was the southern Irish Queen Mab.

In 1815 the tradition of Clan "Tartans" appeared – chiefly under the guidance of the oxymoronically named "Highland Society of London" - Scottish traditions, and history, was being redesigned, rewritten, co-ordinated and documented by individuals living hundreds of miles outside of Scotland.

The Scottish novelist, Sir Walter Scott wrote the Waverley novel, and about the "Highland Robin Hood" Rob Roy MacGregor, and for good measure, discovered the long lost Scottish crown. He also helped to formulate the image we have of the archetypal Scot, ready for the visit of George IV to Edinburgh in 1822. In the minds eye it is a very pretty image of a Scot – a bold rugged highlander, long red hair blowing in the wind, the pleats of his chequered kilt swirling around his body, his dirk in one hand, claymore and targe in the other, as he stares out across the water to his ancient homeland in Ireland. The snow capped mountains in the background contrasting with the "bonnie purple heather". It's a shortbread tin version of History, hard to shift from the mind, and aspirational. Just for good measure he also helped create the ridiculous "ancient Highland costume" that George IV wore for his visit to Edinburgh.

In 1832, William Skene, the son of James Skene, a friend of the same Sir Walter Scott, wrote *"The Highlanders of Scotland, their Origin, History and Antiquities"* and the link of Highlanders to ancient Scots from Ireland was fixed academically. The "Irish" Scot now belongs to the Western Highlands and Argyll. "True" Scots are now the bold men of the West Highlands.

Something else was also happening in the 19th century. The Empire was getting larger. The Aristocracy, Industrialists and the educated middle classes were getting richer from their new possessions across the globe. And the new Empire was being driven from London, and being forged in England's name, not in the name of "The United Kingdom of Great Britain and Ireland ". In the popular press and across the world, Queen Victoria, the monarch of Great Britain & Ireland, was referred to as the Queen of England, and the Empire, it's possessions and the people of Britain were all "English".

The Scottish upper classes, and some parts of the population accepted the new status of Scotland, but others were unhappy. In the 18th century this dissatisfaction had been masked by memories and fear of the brutal impact of the 17th century Covenanters resistance to Episcopalianism, the Jacobite rebellions of 1715 and 1745, martial law and subsequent concerns over the possible return of "Catholic" Stuart monarchs, and the American War of Independence – but as the century had drawn to a close, it was starting to emerge from the shadows. It can be seen in the behaviour of some radical individuals of the time – Robert Burns' *"parcel of Rogues"* statement, his open support for the

French Revolution and political reform. In the 19th century, this dissatisfaction resurfaced politically, the demand rose for self-government, culminating in the Scottish Home Rule movement of 1853, with further demands occurring in 1913, 1930, 1949, 1979 and the rise of Scottish National Party from the 1960's onwards. In an unsuccessful attempt to placate the demand for Home Rule, the Scottish Office was created in 1885 to promote and protect Scotland's interests. There were "criminal" acts in the 20th Century - the theft of the Stone of Destiny from Westminster in 1950, and pillar boxes defaced at the start of the reign of Queen Elizabeth II - as the title she took disregarded Scotland's history as an independent realm - only medieval England had had a Queen Elizabeth, there had never been a Queen Elizabeth of Great Britain before.

In 19th century Scotland, a population, or at least a significant part of it, was not happy with with the idea of living in "North Britain", government from London, and no voice in the future of their country. It's upper, political and educated classes were the exact opposite, fully engaged with being North British, and desiring further integration. This class encouraged the teaching of English History in schools. And they got their way - from the 1700's up to the 1980's the history of the Kings and Queens of Medieval England were being taught in Scottish schools - very little or nothing at all, was being taught about Scottish Kings and Queens.

It was the educated classes, of 19th & 20th century Scotland, that determined the direction of Scottish history. They supported the "Anglo Saxon model" of British History, and to "muddy the waters", there was another development that many of these "educated classes" supported, the - now discredited - theory of Eugenics. A corruption of Charles Darwin's work, where the strongest mate together, to create a "superbreed". In the version of history they used to justify this nonsense, they saw the Germanic tribes of the Dark Ages as the "strongest" race, succeeding the Romans, conquering most of Europe and replacing the previous incumbents. English was seen as the language of Anglo-Saxons, rather than the hybrid language it is. For the educated classes, if Lowland Scots spoke English, the Anglo-Saxon tribes must have conquered Scotland.

To prove it Bede, Gildas, Nennius, and multiple Medieval Irish, English and Scottish histories are re-read, re-translated & Tudor era histories come out of the woodwork, including Bishop John Leslie's incorrectly placed Donbriton. Adomnan talked of Columba's visit to Rhydderich of Strathclyde, and the ancient kings of Strathclyde were found in an ancient Welsh source – the Annales Cambrie *Y Cymmrodor,* so Strathclyde must be Welsh. Strathclyde in spite of all of the Gaelic placenames (and now the archaeological evidence) is seen as a Welsh Kingdom – a land of "Britons". Bede's Gulf of the Sea is pushed forward to the Clyde and Dumbarton becomes Alcluith – even though neither the Clyde nor Dumbarton actually fit. The likes of William Skene have to justify a name change and corrupt the words of Bede to make it fit – at no point did Bede claim Alcluith was ever called a "fortress of the Britons". And for the East Coast, Bede talks of a rather obscure 7th century English King, Edwin of Northumbria, for whom Edinburgh was named after, this was in spite of the Gaelic name for Edinburgh appearing as *Din Edin*, in the 6th century poem "Y Goddodin" by Aineirin. The East Coast of the Lowlands is now occupied by Angles from Bernicia. Edinburgh "the Athens of the North", the "capital" of Scotland, it's political, judicial and economic heart, is an "Anglo-Saxon" city in an "Anglo-Saxon" region. The fact that Lothian, derives from the Votadini tribe, a mere detail.

West Highlanders are now the "Irish" Scots. West Lowlanders are "Welsh", East Lowlanders are "English", and the Picts are the enigma. They have to occupy the North East as there is nowhere else, they can't be Vikings because Vikings never settled there, the only option left was that they were indigenous. A very dubious practice was taking place when Historians were looking for supporting evidence – picking and choosing which parts of Adomnan, Bede, Gildas, Nennius etc to use. Historians were happy to have Saxon invaders from Germany, Scots from Ireland but not happy to have Picts from Scythia, with "Irish wives".

In the process Scotland becomes a microcosm of Britain, a land containing all of the peoples of Britain. The theory is unchallenged and brings a benefit for the educated and political classes. The majority of "Scots" are no longer really Scots – they are either Welsh or English, with just a smattering of Irish and Indigenous DNA, why wouldn't they just accept themselves as Britons. In the process they create anomalies such as the ones below that no-one appears to challenge.

a) Lack of Archaeological evidence - Ancient Scots coming to Argyll in the $5^{th}/6^{th}$ century, that leave no trace whatsoever.

b) Scots that aren't Scots, Gaels that aren't Gaels – Highlanders called themselves Albannach – they never referred to themselves as Scots.

c) Gaelic place-names in the wrong location - A Strathclyde "welsh" kingdom populated with Gaelic place-names, some relating to early Irish saints – Kilmarnock (St Mernoc – from the voyage of St Brendan), Kilmalcolm, Kilwinning, Troon, Ardrossan, Irvine, Girvan, Stranraer, Ayr, Daly, Dalrymple, even Glasgow etc. A new term was created to answer the problem – Gallovidian Gaelic, spoken from Galloway to Carrick. A new language is invented for Cumbrians – Cimbric, not mentioned by Bede, Nennius or anyone else living at that time. But Cimbric, i.e. Brythonic, shows evidence of Gaelic influence which can only come from a relationship with lowland Scotland and Irish settlers living there - Scots.

d) The wrong language being spoken in the wrong place - A Strathclyde "Welsh" Kingdom speaking English by the end of the 11th century, that was "conquered" sometime between 1018 and 1054 by "Scots", but with no known battle ever having taken place. It is filled with Gaelic place-names, that show evidence of continuous occupation from at least the 3rd/4th centuries AD. "Welsh" speakers until 1018, switch to Gaelic and finally English in less than a century. - less than 2 generations. For good measure they manage to "time travel" and give 3/4th century settlements Gaelic names. A ridiculous situation, it takes hundreds of years for a language to alter, not a single generation jump. Gaelic was spoken from the very earliest, probably pre-Roman period.

e) Unique place-names not in unique locations - An ancient "fort of the Britons" (Dumbarton) that was neither ancient nor unique, in a land supposedly populated with Britons and multiple ancient settlements, including other hill forts – what would make Dumbarton really stand out as a fort of the "Britons".

f) Welsh speaking Irishmen - A Strathclyde kingdom, trading with and being populated continuously from the 6th century BC - 1st century AD, That's 700 years of continuous settlement from Ireland, why exactly would Irish settlers be speaking "Welsh" ?.

g) Unique Ethnic characteristics not in unique locations - A

13th century hero William Wallace, whose forebears settled in Strathclyde around the 11th/12th century, and whose surname originated because they were "Welsh" - why would a Welshman stand out in a kingdom populated with "Welshmen".

The anomalies are left unquestioned, the perpetrators lauded for their brilliance, Dark Ages are rediscovered, Arthurian legends popularised. "Druidism", or rather Pseudo-Druidism is reinvented – with mystical sounding incantations that, in reality, were created in the Victorian mind, owing more to smoke & mirrors than ancient Celts.

The "medieval" Pict, portraits of tattooed naked men and women, appears again. Their world is mysterious, savage, with ancients Gods, Druids, Stone Circles like the Ring of Brodgar. (and Stonehenge). They have strange, magical figures painted onto their bodies and ceremonies taken from ancient biblical lands such as Scythia, Thracia, Phonecia, Egypt. The Pict takes centre stage, attention is deflected away from the Scots, and academic challenges to the "accepted" view of ancient Scottish History are not made when archaeological evidence starts to mount up. studies concentrate on solving the "mysteries" of these ancient "prehistoric" people,.

In the latter 20th Century, the Pict is a "tourist" industry. People flock to carved stones, with images of "Gods". There are coach & train trips to ancient monuments, hotels booked, museum fees paid, gifts & books bought and sold. Replicas and Ornaments made. Books are published in their hundreds. It's a commercial enterprise – not bad going for a term that just means a British Barbarian.

Summary

The Native Tribes in Northern Britain were divided into 3 main groups during the Roman Occupation. The way the tribes were divided is outlined at the start of the Pictish Chronicle.

They were a mixed bag of tribes from various European origins with a leadership probably drawn from La Tene Era Celts. The Romans named the first 2 groups from a native language, meaning a "tribe" - Pict – Some tribes of Cruithne – Verturiones, Some tribes from An - Britain (An) – the Dicalydones. The term Pict became a reference for a British Barbarian. The other groups from, an Irish origin, that joined them became known as Scots. In the south of England the Romans used local tribes of Germanic origin and possibly brought in some more to help control the local population. Amongst the regions that these groups occupied there existed "pockets" of unrelated tribes, from many different backgrounds.

At some point the Romano-British – the new group of mixed Roman educated "British" living in the towns and cities of Roman Britain, found a sense of "Britishness" and identified themselves as Britons, writing down the History of Britain as relating to themselves only. Instead of being conquered by the Romans, their history saw themselves as allies and sometimes superior to the Romans. Helen, the mother of the first Christian Emperor Constantine becomes a Briton, King Arthur *"conquers Gaul"* and *"invades Rome"*. The Romano-British reinvented their history. The Picts, "the barbarian native British tribes" didn't fit this model and became "strangers from a foreign land".

During the period from the 5th - 10th century, there are a number of changes taking place. The Celtic church, under the direction of Irish monks, gradually assumes the religious control of North of Britain. The Gallic Church, control of Southern Britain.

The impact of this is that the "Irish" tribes on the south west coast of Scotland become pre-eminent. The old Gods disappear and inspired by an "Irish" religious vision, a "new" fashion takes place. Instead of the old word "Pict" the Irish version becomes pre-eminent – Scot. The tribes of Northern Britain transform their history and become a mix of Irish and "Pictish" tribes – to be fair they probably that anyway.

They've already been converted to Christianity by Irish monks, their family names, local place-names don't change. Essentially other than a change at the "top", the switch is pretty painless. Hence the rapidity with which the word "Pict" disappears.

Chances are the Picts never really had any real attachment to the name themselves anyway. It just meant a barbarian British tribe – nothing more, they may not even have recognised that they were "Picts". The use of the name all depends on perspective. The Picts were always someone else, always the "Bad Guys". At various times dependant on the various allegiances that were forged, it was probably never clear what exactly who they were – they were probably, Scot, Briton, Pict, Saxon at different times – just depended on who was writing, and who was in charge at the time, hence in 778AD, the death is reported of Eilpin, king of Saxons, but really this was Alpin, King of Picts.

In the medieval period, the Picts come back – in literacy anyway – they took on a new identity, following the discoveries in the Americas, The native American princess Pocahontas, becomes famous for saving John Smith, she marries John Rolfe, and is entertained by the Stuart monarchy,. A fashion for the native and exotic, and a search for one of our very own - the "British" Savage.

The Pict satisfied the desire for a native exotic British "Savage", they became the old people of Britain. Artists started drawing the Pict warrior with woad warpaint, running around naked in strange prehistoric rituals - our version of the American native. When the early Pictish stones were found, instead of Communication, they saw "Totem Poles".

This vision of a "British Savage" became compounded in the Victorian Era. A fascination for mysticism, fantasies and fairy tales meant many learned men, such as Sir Arthur Conan Doyle – a practising Doctor and famous writer – got caught up in the fantasy world of fortune telling and fairies.

Pseudo-religions such as Druidism, attempts to recreate the past by constructing Follies, Confidence tricks, Monsters, ancient made-up tongues became common place. The image of the Pict from medieval times fitted into this fantasy.

In reality there was a very significant difference between the Picts and the indigenous people that were discovered during the "Voyages of Discoveries" from the 15th century onwards. The Native Americans, Maories, Aborigines were stone age peoples, they lived in lands that were remote and inaccessible, developing civilisations couldn't reach them. The Picts didn't, they went through the bronze age, iron age built hill forts, the same as everyone else in Britain and Europe, they lived in a very accessible island and there was nothing to stop the Roman army from going to war with them, or any British tribe mingling with them, either before, during or after the Roman occupation.

Pict was just a word – we use it for a race of people. Everyone else used it to mean a native British tribe.

Bibliography (& Suggested Reading)

Perceptions of the Picts;
From Eumenius to John Buchan
Ann Ritchie
A4 Press Inverness
Produced by Groam House Museum
1993

Albion: A Guide to Legendary Britain
Jennifer Westwood
Harper Collins
1994

The Age of the Picts
W. A. Cummins
Alan Sutton
1995

The Celts
Nora Chadwick
Penguin Books
1991

Celtic: Myths and Legends
T. W. Rolleston
Senate

Classical Dictionary
John Lempriere
Bracken Books
1994

A Dictionary of Irish Mythology
Peter B. Ellis
Oxford University Press
1992

British and Irish Mythology
John & Caitlin Matthews
Diamond Books
1995

The Picts and the Scots
LLoyd & Jenny Laing
Alan Sutton
1995

King Arthur - The True Story
G. Philips& M. Keatman
Arrow
1993
Warlords and Holy Men

Chronicles of Henry of Huntingdon
Bohns Antiquarian Library
Thomas Forrester A.M.
Woodfall and Kinder
London

Zosimus – Historia Nova
London: Green and Chaplin
1814

Nennius
History of the Britons
Translated J. A. Giles
In parentheses Publications
Medieval Latin Series
Ontario
2000

Various translations including:-
Annals of Tighernach
Synchronisms of Fland Mainistrech
Annals of Ulster
Chronicon Scottorum
The Irish version of the Historia Britonum of
Nennius
St Patrick Confessio

Ecclesiastical History of the English People
Bede
Translation by Leo Sherley Price
Penguin Books
1990

De Excidio Britonium
Gildas
Translation by Michael Winterbottom
Phillimore
1978

Life of Columba
Adomnan
Translated by Richard Sharpe
Penguin Books
1995

Early Sources of Scottish History
A. O. Anderson

Chronicles relating to Scotland
Sir Herbert Maxwell
John MacLehose& Sons

165

Alfred P. Smith
Edinburgh University Press
1995

An Illustrated History of Ireland
Mary F. Cusack
Bracken Books
1995

Scotland: A New History
Michael Lynch
Century
1991

Ulster: An Illustrated History
Edited By C. Brady et al
December
1988

Folk Heroes of Britain
Charles Knightly
Thames and Hudson
1982

Dictionary of National Biography
Various

The Celtic Sources for The Arthurian Legend
John B. Coe & Simon Young
Llanerch
1995

Online resources
Wikipedia
World Populations Growth
Dunnichen Stone
Aberlemno Stone
Norries Law Hoarde

1912

The Conquest of Gaul
Caesar
Translated by S. A. Handford
Penguin Books
1982

The History of the Kings of Britain
Geoffrey of Monmouth
Translated by Lewis Thorpe
Penguin Books
1966

The Agricola
Tacitus
Translated by H. Mattingly
Penguin Books
1970

The Later Roman Empire
Ammianus Marcellinus
Translated by W. Hamilton
Penguin Books
1986

The Anglo-Saxon Chronicles
Translated by Anne Savage
Colour Library Books
1995

A History of the Kings of England
Simeon of Durham
Translated by J. Stephenson
Llanerch
1987

Online Sources :
Maps - Wikipedia/National Library of Scotland/British library etc.
http://www.historicalarts. co.uk/articles/sinsear/the_birth_of_lugh.html)
http://web.onetel.net.uk/~hibou/Pictish Inscriptions.html
https://en.wikipedia.org/wiki/World_population_estimates#Deep_prehistory
http://www.worldhistorysite.com/population.html
https://en.wikipedia.org/wiki/European_ Americans
http://www.electricscotland.com/history/early4-1.htm
http://penelope.uchicago.edu/Thayer/E/Gazetteer/Periods/Roman/_Texts/Ptolemy/2/2*.html#Vindogara_town
http://www.helensburgh-heritage.co.uk/index.php?option=com_content&view=article&id=1384:roman-harbour-discovered
http://orkneyjar.com/history/earlyrefs.htm
https://upload.wikimedia.org/wikipedia/commons/e/e6/Ptolemy_Cosmographia_1467_-_Great_Britain_and_Ireland.jpg

Made in the USA
Coppell, TX
07 November 2021